Sangama

A Confluence of Art and Culture During the Vijayanagara Period

Edited
by
Nalini Rao

Sangama

A Confluence of Art and Culture During the Vijayanagara Period

Edited
by
Nalini Rao

Originals
(an imprint of Low Price Publications)
Delhi-110052 (India)

Distributed by
D.K. Publishers Distributors (P) Ltd.
4834/24, Ansari Road, Darya Ganj,
New Delhi-110002
Phones: 51562573, 51562575, 51562578
e-mail: dkpd@del3.vsnl.net.in
visit us at: www.dkpd.com

First Published 2006

ISBN 81-88629-48-0

Published by
Originals
(an imprint of Low Price Publications)
A-6, Nimri Commercial Centre,
Near Ashok Vihar Phase-IV, Delhi-110052
Phones: 27302453
e-mail: lpp@nde.vsnl.net.in
visit us at: www.lppindia.com

Printed at
D K Fine Art Press P Ltd.
Delhi-110052

PRINTED IN INDIA

Contents

Preface

Works on Vijayanagara in the form of books, monographs, and articles have appeared in immense quantity in recent years. The expanding research on the city and empire of Vijayanagara in South India has generated numerous theories and inspired new questions into the workings of Vijayanagara society and the cultural phenomena. The present volume provides a micro-level understanding of the polity, society and art of the Vijayanagara period which stretched for three centuries, from the fourteenth till the seventeenth centuries.

This book is published in conjunction with the seminar, Sangama: A Confluence of Art and Culture during the Vijayanagara Period, 2005. The title of the seminar emanates from the first dynasty of kings who reigned the kingdom from (c. 1336 C.E.- c. 1565 C.E.). But the primary goal of this endeavor is to comprehend *sangama* as the confluence of social, cultural and artistic forces. The other objective is to explore the continuity of the dynamic links which emanated before Vijayanagara and continued over succeeding generations. The idea of *sangama* is expanded to include more than dualistic categories of royal and sacred, city and empire, village and urban; it encompasses interrelated domains and links between pluralistic forces that are woven into a broad reunifying landscape of surviving monuments. The set of essays selected here, explore patterns of interaction, modes of operations of main and intermediate groups and communities and the relational concepts that led to the chiseling of articulations on monumental temples, imperial structures and building of tanks and gateways. These were visual forms of power especially those of social and religious exchange as well as political and cultural continuities.

Each author was asked to write on a topic related to his or her research and to apply this research to Vijayanagara. The result is a wide variety of topics, some specifically on Vijayanagara, others more broadly on South India, but all that ultimately tell us how religious, artistic, and political traditions intertwined during the fourteenth to seventeenth centuries. Much of the hard evidence at Vijayanagara is now available: archaeological, art historical, inscriptional, and textural. The articles included in this volume have attempted to use this evidence to tease out trajectories of cultural change, stasis, and hybridity. One point they all appear to suggest is that Vijayanagara was a center of complex interweaving of influences, a few threads of which are brought out in these papers.

Robert L. Brown introduces us to the current theories and interpretations based on archaeological evidences. He considers the period as an important transitional phase for formalization of a new political order and royal patronage to temples which were centers of power. He accords sufficient importance to the theory of 'Hinduness' as an inspiration both for the founding of the empire as well as for a continuous process of political and religious integration which was taking place.

Nagaraja Rao provides an introduction to the empire and city of Vijayanagara and the significant archaeological finds in the recent excavations conducted in the city. He discusses the role of the Hampi Project undertaken to preserve this world heritage site.

Anila Verghese' paper is a valuable and exhaustive analysis of the evolution of Vijayanagara pillars and its continuity and transformation in the Nayaka period.

Choodamani Nandagopal describes the complex interrelation between transformation of religious ideas and institutions and changes in sculpture and music due to *bhakti* movement and royal patronage.

Gerard Foekema makes a detailed study of architectural orders, especially the Nagara and Dravida forms and its synthesis in three Late Chalukyan temples, which helps us understand the creative changes during the period under review.

Nalini Rao focuses upon the tactics of royal gifting to religious institutions which formed the basis of network alliances between three major institutions, the king, temple and the guild. The essay utilizes artistic evidences to understand the economic powers of gifting in sustaining an urban economy and its symbolic values of legitimacy and power relationship.

Deepak Shimkhada discusses the bhakti aspect of the new reform movement of Veershaivism and interlinks it with concepts about Shiva, temple and idolatory that influenced the development of South Indian religious and social culture.

S.R.Rao explores the contribution of Sayana to Sanskrit Vedic studies during the period under review and the role of *agrahāras* as educational institutions.

Subhash Kak explains the theory of numbers found in sacred Hindu temple architecture by using cosmological concepts embedded in Vedic literature and relates them to buildings and material objects in Indus Valley Civilization.

Aparna Raghunatha and Amita Sinha examine the case of the Rockfort temple at Tiruchirapalli and argue for need of conservation of sacred landscape to become an urban planning and design tool in India.

Indu Parthasarthy's writing is centered upon the multiple sources and intermingling of architectural traditions in South India with particular emphasis on the Vidyashankara temple in Shringeri.

We have attempted to interest both the scholar and the general reader about the richness and educative value of Indian studies with a deep faith in their continued interest and inspiration. But only the reader can judge whether this book achieves the coherence and contribution that we desire from it. Whatever his judgement, we wish to thank the authors for agreeing to embark on such a project which was hastily put together; I am grateful to them for their willing responsiveness to send us their scholarly essays in a very short period of time. I would like to express a special debt to my teacher, Dr. R.L. Brown for his suggestions and constant inspiration.

This volume and the seminar is the product of the enthusiasm of Vatsa Kumar, President of Kannada Vrinda, Houston, Texas. He has been associated with Kannada Vrinda since the day one of its founding in 1983. I thank him for his dedication and untiring efforts to bring out this volume on time and organizing the educative seminar in Houston and Los Angeles in November 2005. I would like to thank the publisher, Pradeep Mittal of Originals (an imprint of Low Price Publications), for agreeing to publish this volume within a short time to be released at the seminar. Finally, we are grateful and honored by the generosity and enthusiasm of all Kannadigas for their support.

Nalini Rao

1

Vijayanagara: The End or the Beginning?

Robert L. Brown

Few archaeological sites in India have received as much attention as Vijayanagara. The scholarly bibliography on the site is enormous and ever expanding. There are now many good introductions to the site with its art, architecture, religion, and history being discussed within a variety of scholarly disciplines. Vijayanagara has served the academic community so well in part because it was destroyed so completely in c.1565 C.E. While this may sound paradoxical, the looting and burning of the city following the defeat of the Vijayanagara army led to its abandonment. What stood at the time were the many brick and stone structures. While stripped of their movable treasures in metals and gems, and the wood structures reduced to ash, much was preserved until the present day. The constant rebuilding and alterations that would have taken place had the site been continuously inhabited did not take place. In addition, the period when the site prospered was recorded in extensive textual and inscriptional references, including sources in a variety of Indian languages (Telegu, Kannada, Tamil), as well as some of the earliest and most detailed descriptions by European visitors to an Indian city. Adding to this wealth of artistic and textual information has been the extensive archaeological research and publications by teams of scholars over the last two decades. Among these scholars are M.S. Nagaraja Rao, Vasundhara Filliozat, Pierre Filliozat, George Michelle, and John Fritz, and as they have uncovered and published more and more of the material and textual evidence at Vijayanagara, they have proposed interpretations of the city's uses, meanings, and characteristics, so that today we tend to see the site through their eyes.

The current scholarly interpretation is that the site was divided into two centers, a royal center and a sacred center. These two centers were separated by agricultural and urban areas, and the entire complex was surrounded by rings of defensive walls and gates. The royal and sacred centers are interpreted as exemplary of a cosmic city, one in which the king and the deity interrelate in ritual acts of worship and public displays of theater. Vijayanagara is regarded as an ideal Hindu city, one in which sculpture, architecture, and urban planning are used to create power and meaning by linking Hindu gods and earthly kings.

It is the 'Hinduness' of Vijayanagara that is its most important feature, and is the characteristic that is constantly being reevaluated and rethought by scholars. Perhaps the most popular interpretation of Vijayanagara is as a Hindu bulwark against the expansion in the fifteenth and sixteenth centuries of the Muslim sultanates. The expansion of Muslim political control toward the south eventually put during the Mughal period most of the subcontinent under Islamic rule. The view of Vijayanagara as holding back Muslim expansion is not inaccurate, although it accentuates the Hindu versus Muslim dichotomy which divides pre-modern South Asia into two distinct parts according to religion. The political and cultural reality is, of course, much more complex than two contending monolithic religions, and the ways in which Hindus and Muslims interacted at Vijayanagara are the focus of considerable scholarship, which has not been without surprising conclusions.

Such discussions can sometimes show us what about the city, and more broadly the kingdom, was part of a previous historical, artistic, and religious tradition, and what was in fact innovative and new. We can ask if Vijayanagara was the end of a long medieval development of Hindu culture in India, a final blossoming that was snuffed out upon the disastrous defeat by Islamic armies in c. 1565 C.E. At times it appears that Vijayanagara was a new beginning, whereas even though the city itself was looted and abandoned, the economic, political, and cultural foundations were laid for what was to become early modern India. A third viewpoint is that the city was neither the end of a tradition, nor the beginning of a new one, but something of a transition between the old and the new.

The traditional story of Vijayanagara's beginnings speaks of two brothers, Hukka and Bukka, founding the city in c. 1336 C.E., an act that involved the brothers returning to their Hindu faith by denouncing their conversion to Islam. Thus, the birth of the city was an act of defiance against the Islamic rulers and an assertion of the city as Hindu. This story, while probably not historically accurate, does clearly set out the ideology that the rulers of Vijayanagara will follow for the next two hundred years. Archaeological and art historical evidence at the site shows that what was to become the city was occupied from at least the tenth or eleventh centuries with Hindu temples built in the architectural traditions of the Deccan. These temples are focused on the small Hemakuta hill, near the Tungabhadra River. It is around this early sacred hill that Vijayanagara's sacred center will grow, while most of the important temple complexes will be constructed following the Tungabhadra. The centrality of the Hindu temple to Vijayanagara, both as a city site as well as the center of kingdom, continued throughout its existence, and can be part of the argument both for interpreting the site as the end of medieval Indian traditions as well as new beginnings.

The royal center was built south of the sacred center, and was the house of the king. It too, however, was centered on a Hindu temple, the Ramachandra temple, literally placed at the center of the palace buildings. Following again the arguments of John Fritz and others, the royal center was divided by a north/south axis that separated the royal center into two halves, a private residence to the east, and a public area for performances and rituals to the west. The Ramachandra temple pierced this axis so that it connected both the private and public royal arenas. Indeed, the homology of the king and the deity, Rama becomes apparent with the home of the king and of the god in one structure. Thus, the *dharmic* nature of Hindu kingship reaches its perfection at Vijayanagara, and the Hindu temple becomes the template for the city and kingdom.

During the fifteenth and sixteenth centuries at Vijayanagara and in South India, the Hindu temple is changing its role, style, and patronage, all of which point ahead to what will follow in pre-modern India. Somewhat paradoxically, considering that the importance of the Hindu temple is if anything iṣ accentuating during these centuries, the general thrust of change is toward a kind of secularization. It is during these centuries that European contact with Italians and Portuguese becomes important, some of whom left detailed descriptions of Vijayanagara. These Europeans were priests, adventurers and soldiers, but above all merchants, and they introduced new technologies associated with warfare. Indeed, warfare was a constant feature of Vijayaganara political and social life, and it was not only with Muslim adversaries, but also with Hindus that the Vijayanagara kings did battle. The importance of European weapons and, above all, imported horses to the Vijayanagara kings cannot be overly stressed. But the point here is that the interaction with European merchants, and more broadly with the Indian mercantile communities, created a fairly diverse and open social environment, one that we might speak of today as being multicultural.

This diversity and tolerance can be seen in other areas of Vijayanagara culture. We know from European descriptions and from the archaeological and art historical evidence that there were sizable communities of Muslims and Jains, as well as Hindus, at Vijayanagara. And even within the Hindu groups, there was an openness to various non-Brahmanical strains, including an absorption of folk deities that were very popular, their cults based on oral teachings and village worship. It was during these centuries, not surprisingly, that more and more vernacular languages were used for religious texts throughout India, opening Hindu theology, rituals, and stories to an ever more popular audience.

The religious and cultural tolerance and ecumenism were accompanied by an increasing social mobility. Here the Hindu temple continued its central political role, serving as a locus for integrating groups of people into new environments. Several scholars have explored how the Hindu temples during this period served as mechanisms for economic investment and agricultural planning. The ability of groups of people, often of a particular caste or *jāti*, to move by using the temples to integrate them into new geographical areas, even to areas in which their language was not dominant, seems surprising, yet their mobility fits with that of the merchants and even the armies. While the fifteenth and sixteenth centuries cannot be seen as a time of peace and security, it was a time when people accepted difference and innovation as a way to deal with change, producing a type of secularity.

The sculpture on the temples at Vijayanagara also undergoes change at this time. There is a sharp increase in the amount of portrait sculpture. This increase may be tied in part to a change in temple and artistic patronage, as more and more non-royal individuals and groups become patrons. The subject of the relief sculptures also begins to show more secular scenes, such as on the famous Mahanavami Dibba platform with its rows of dancing women, horses, athletes, and soldiers. These figures are not actors in a story of Hindu deities, but are meant to be representatives of the actual Vijayanagara populace who celebrated the royal rituals and participated in the king's public displays of honor and legitimation. These figures are among the first secular subjects found in Indian art.

Only a few of the social and religious changes that we glimpse at Vijayanagara have been suggested here, but one can see that it was a period of important innovations that will find their impact long after the site was abandoned. While the Hindu character of Vijayanagara is the site's most important characteristic, and the Hindu temple its organizational center, the city was a dynamic locus of rapid, sometimes startling, change and adaptation to a newly forming Indian society. As such, Vijayanagara can be regarded as both a blossoming of the past Hindu traditions, and a source for new traditions that will arise in the future to deal with a changing world.

The essay is based on the ideas and scholarship of a number of scholars, some of whom are named in the text. A key collection of articles on Vijayanagara that was published in 1985 remains one of the most fruitful in terms of ideas regarding the site: *Vijayanagara—City and Empire: New Currents of Research,* 2 vols., edited by Anna Libera Dallapiccola (Stuttgart:

Steiner Verlag Wiesbaden). John Fritz and George Michell have published a number of studies, often with very helpful descriptions of buildings and other features of the built environment with plans and elevations. Particularly helpful is *City of Victory* (New York: Aperture, 1991). A series of volumes, each with separate titles and authors, has been published as part of the Vijayanagara Research Project Monograph Series.

2

Recent Excavations in Vijayanagara: A Word Heritage Site

M.S. Nagaraja Rao

The founding of the Vijayanagara empire by Harihara and Bukka in c.1336 C.E. changed the political and cultural history of South India. The powerful Hindu kingdom, has left an impressive mark in the capital of Vijayanagara (Hampi) in the form of a large fortified city. Here are numerous large palaces, temple cities, bazaars, gateways, shrines and images which have helped historians reconstruct this medieval capital. Archaeologists have brought to light innumerable structures, such as palaces, platforms, tanks, walls, gateways and pottery. Excavations conducted by our team led by George Michell and John Fritz have led us to view the city as consisting of two major zones, the Royal and Sacred. I have briefly described some of the material remains which have been unearthed, discussed the role of the Hampi Resurrection Project and enunciated the need for further excavation, documentation, conservation and research.

Vijayanagara Rulers

The kingdom of Vijayanagara (c.1336-1565 C.E.) was ruled by four successive dynasties, the Sangamas, Saluvas, Tuluvas and Aravidus who checked the onslaught of Islam, especially from the Bahamani kingdom which was to remain the chief enemy of Vijayanagara almost throughout its history. It was founded by in c. 1336 C.E. by two Sangama brothers, Harihara and Bukka who were who were probably feudatories under the

Hoysalas. The city was named Vijayanagara, the city of victory, in honor of the sage Vidyaranya. The brothers occupied the region south of river Tungabhadra, near the Virupaksha temple. Bukka was succeeded by Harihara II (c.1376 C.E.- c. 1404 C.E.) who assumed imperial titles of *mahārajādhirāja* and *rājaparameshwara* and undertook a number of military campaigns, establishing river Krishna as the northern boundary of the Vijayanagara kingdom. He was succeeded by Virupaksa I (c. 1404 C.E.- c. 1406 C.E.) and later by Devaraya I (c. 1406 C.E.- c. 1422 C.E.) and subsequently by Devaraya II, when the Italian traveler, Nicolo di Conti, (c.1420 C.E.- c. 1421 C.E.) and Abdur Razaaq (c. 1442 C.E.), the Persian ambassador, visited the city, both of whom have left written accounts of the kingdom. Saluva Narasimha (c.1486-1493 C.E.) who established the Saluva family of kings was followed briefly by Immadi Narasimha (c. 1491C.E.- c. 1492 C.E.). The reign of Immadi Narasimha ended when his regent and general Narasa Nayaka (c. 1492-1503 C.E.) who usurped the throne thereby beginning the Tuluva family of rulers. After his death, his place was taken by his son, Immadi Narasa Nayaka, better known as Veera Narasimha (c. 1505 C.E.- c. 1509 C.E.). After a brief reign of five years he bequeathed the throne to his step brother, Krishnadevaraya.

Krishnadevaraya (c. 1509 C.E.- c. 1530 C.E.) was one of the most accomplished rulers of Vijayanagara. Having recaptured Goa, incorporated Sivasamudra, Golkunda, Kondaveedu and Kondapalli, the kingdoms of the Cholas, Pandyas and Cheras, he undertook brilliant military campaigns against the Gajapatis of Orissa in the east; thereby extending his kingdom from the river Krishna to Cape Comorin. In c.1530 C.E., Krishnadevaraya was succeeded by his step brother Achyutaraya (c. 1530 C.E. - c. 1542 C.E.) during whose time Fernao Nuniz visited Vijayanagara (c. 1533-c. 1537 C.E.). For twenty years (c.1543 C.E.- c.1563 C.E.) the empire flourished under his successor, Veera Sadashivaraya who died in battle and was succeeded by Tirumala. However, in c. 1565 C.E., the combined Moslem armies of Ahmadnagar, Golcunda and Bijapur defeated Tirumalaraya in the battle of Raksasi-Tangdi (also referred to as the battle of Talikota). Tirumalaraya escaped, leaving Vijayanagara to be ransacked by the armies of the Sultans.

Presently, this magnificent medieval capital lies in its ruined condition. We are confronted only with ruins, consisting of remains of buildings that were once temples and palaces, bazaars and massive walls that constituted its defenses. Even the name, Vijayanagara, has faded out of our memory, and the remains are known as Hampi Ruins lying near the village of Hampi.

Description of the City

Vijayanagara occupies an extensive area on the southern banks of the river Tungabhadra in the Hospet Taluk of Bellary District in the State of Karnataka. It was located in picturesque surroundings, amidst lofty hills of granite, with nature at its wildest. The site is naturally endowed with great strategic strength. The wide, torrential river Tungabhadra and the impassable craggy granite hills, provided strong natural defenses which the rulers used to their advantage. The Vijayanagara kings constructed seven walls of fortification around the city which contained palaces, roads, markets, temples, agricultural areas and even a hydraulic system. It was a heavily populated city and as the foreign visitor, Abdur Razaaq writes:

> "The city of Bidjanagar is such that the pupil of the eye has never seen a place like it, and the ear intelligence has never been informed that there existed anything to equal it in the world."[1]

Vijayanagara was visited by several foreign travelers who have all left a description of the grandeur of the city which they saw. They have provided a graphic description of its structures, customs, rituals, festivals, celebrations, court life and important contemporary events. Among the accounts are those by Portuguese travelers, Domingo Paes and Fernao Nuniz, the Persian ambassador, Abdur Razaaq and Italian traveler, Nicolo di Conti, and Duarte Barbosa. Abdur Razaaq, who visited Vijayanagara in c. 1442 C.E. during the reign of Deva Raya II was fascinated by its wealth and has left us a detailed account of the capital, especially about the *mahānavami* (*dasara*) festival which should be told in his own words:

> "In pursuance of orders issued by the king of Bidjanagar, the generals and principal personages from all parts of his empire presented themselves at the palace. During three consecutive days in the month of Redjeb the vast space of land magnificently decorated, in which the enormous elephants were congregated together, presented the appearance of the waves of the sea...Over this magnificent space were erected numerous pavilions, to the height of three, four, or even five storeys, covered from top to bottom with figures in relief. In the front of his palace rose a place with nine pavilions magnificently ornamented. In the ninth the throne was set up. In the seventh was allotted a place to the humble author of this narrative. Between the palace and the pavillions were musicians and story-tellers."[2]

Domingo Paes, the Portuguese traveler, who visited Vijayanagara in c. 1520 C.E. describes the bazaar:

> "You have a broad and beautiful street, full of rows of fine houses and streets of the sorts I have described, and it is to be understood that the houses belong to men rich enough to afford such. In this street lived many merchants, and there you will find all sorts of rubies, and diamonds, and emeralds and pearls, and seed- pearls, and clothes, and every other sort of thing there is on earth that you may wish to buy....this is the best provided city in the world."[3]

Nicolo di Conti, who visited Vijayanagara in c.1420 C.E., gives an account of the celebrations,[4] while the Italian visitor, Ludovico de Varthema, provides information about the customs and conditions during Vijayanagara times.[5] Portugues Fray Luis who visited Vijayanagara on behalf of Alfonso d'Albuquerque, has left a meager account.[6] However, it must also be mentioned that there are a large number of written documents as well, in the form of inscriptions, in Kannada, Telugu and Sanskrit as well as contemporary texts which help us to construct the city.

The Hampi Project

The remains of the imperial city of Vijayanagara are spread over a vast area of about 26 sq.kms. covering several modern villages, while the outer lines of its fortifications include a larger area. The monuments which are popularly known as Hampi Ruins, are mainly situated between the villages of Kamalapuram in the South to Hampi village on the right bank of Tungabhadra in the north. They extend in an area of about 16 kms. radius.

The cultural remains of Hampi have not received the attention they deserve both from the point of view of immense archaeological remains of an imperial capital, and a place of tourist attraction. The foreign visitor is surprised at its extent and grandeur as a ruined city, just as those foreign travelers who visited in the fifteenth and sixteenth centuries. According to them, there is no comparable evidence of archaeological remains of such a great medieval city anywhere in the world. Hence the Government of Karnataka took the right decision to resurrect this city. The research project, now designated Resurrection of Hampi (Vijayanagara) has been drawn up, and is being executed for more than a quarter of a century. The archaeological excavations for more than a quarter of a century at Vijayanagara has been most rewarding. The Resurrection Project has been implemented since 1979 by the Archaeological Survey of India and the Department of Archaeology and Museums in Karnataka and the Karnataka State Archaeology. Contributions by Dr. George Michell, Dr. John Fritz have yielded evidences which have made possible the interpretation of the city as consisting of major zonal areas, the Royal and Sacred.

Royal and Sacred Centers

We have defined the Sacred Center as being in the northern part of the city, along the river Tungabhadra consisting of number of religious structures, especially the temple cities, and the Royal Center in the heart of the city, within the innermost fortifications, consisting of remains of palatial buildings.[7] In between the Sacred Center and Royal Center is located a large enclosure consisting of palatial buildings belonging to the Noblemen. The Sacred

Center is dominated by four large temple complexes: the Virupaksha, Krishna, Tiruvengalanatha (Achyutaraya) and Vitthala temples. These large temple complexes or cities *(puras)* were known by the name of the temple; thus there is the Virupakshapura, Krishnapura, Vitthalapura and Achyutarayapura. The main feature of a *pura* is the large temple complex with its high enclosure walls and towered gateways, approached by a long chariot street flanked on both sides by shops, which functioned as a bazaar.[8]

Excavations in the Sacred Area

Excavations were conducted in the famous Hampi bazaar also known as the Virupaksha bazaar. It was originally 720 meters in length and about 35 meters wide, flanked by *mandapas* or pavilions. The excavations from the eastern end of the bazaar revealed that the original road was paved with stones, a fact which had been recorded by Domingo Paes. A British army officer Col. Sherer who visited Hampi in 1820 exclaimed after seeing the bazaar that he could not believe his eyes. The excavations revealed that the paved road were lined with shops contiguous to one another and according to Abdur Razaak, pearls, rubies, emeralds and diamonds were sold here. However the excavations could not be continued because of the objections of the shop-owners who still occupy the bazaar *mandapas*. The exposed bazaar *mandapas* have now been restored and have been used to exhibit photographs of Hampi taken in 1856 by Col Alexander John Greenlaw.

In the northern part of the Virupaksha temple is the Nagareshwara temple, which was buried under debris. A scientific clearance exposed a debris of three meters depth. The temple was cleared which revealed a paved surface all around; the front hall was dismantled in its entirety and re-erected after strengthening the foundations.

The area known as the Noblemen's Quarters located south of the Hampi bazaar had a natural fortification in the form of granite walls. About eighteen buildings belonging to noblemen have now been excavated and the foundation is exposed. The major structure stands on a high platform within two massive enclosures. This double-storeyed house consists of seven rooms; in front of the house is a square well (still usable) constructed out of dressed stone masonry while on the south-west corner is a water aqueduct. It is interesting to note that while the basement of the structure is built in granite, the superstructure is a wooden construction. We deduced that this was the residence of an important official because the debris of this house yielded Chinese Celedon Ware of the Ming Dynasty. Inmates may have received Chinese visitors who probably brought gifts of porcelain, which was an item of luxury. A similar but slightly smaller structure was excavated to the south- west of the main building and it might have been used as a hall to receive complaints from public. Until now more than eighteen structures have been exposed including a toilet between the houses.

Excavations in the Royal Area

Major discoveries in the royal enclosure include a vast hall, called the Rangashala which could be the hall described by Domingo Paes which he visited with the permission of the king. According to him, here the princesses learnt music and dance and to assist them in the learning process there were sculptures in various dance postures which are described in the *Natyashastra*. Here we find that the interior walls contain niches in which are the remains of stucco figures with their feet in different postures - thus we can identify the hall to be the Rangashala mentioned by Paes. Another important structure that was recently excavated behind the Ramachandra temple is the palace of King Harihara which is confirmed by an inscription plaque, which states in Kannada characters *hariharana aramane*, the palace of king Harihara.

A significant structure which has been unearthed is a stepped tank at the south-west corner of the Mahanavami Dibba. On the surface is a large aqueduct running from east to west with a water chute in the south. Upon excavation, at the end of the water chute, a stepped tank was discovered. The tank is constructed out of pre- fabricated polished chlorite schist, for which the stone is available near Gadag and it is possible that the entire tank was fabricated there. Each stone member had been inscribed upon with a letter in Kannada letter - for *uttara*, a number indicating the horizontal position where the stone has fittings and a *kannada* letter indicating the vertical position of the stone. Its proximity with the Mahanavami Dibba indicates that this was used during the *dasara* festival for ceremonial purposes by the king.

There is yet another interesting structure on the way to river Tungabhadra, the Dharmashala of Ahmed Khan. It was described by Abdur Razaaq as the Moorish quarter of the city and where Islamic tombs have been found. In front of the structure is an octagonal well and on the south side of the structure is the tomb of Ahmed Khan himself. It is a simple plain hall with trefoil arch on the western wall, in the central aisle. The lintel at the central part of the building has a Kannada inscription which states that this Dharmashala was constructed by Kattige Ahmed Khan, a staff bearer of Devaraya so that his lord Devaraya may attain all the merit as long as the sun and the moon exist. He also constructed an octagonal well with the same sense of piety. The three buildings, the Dharamashala, the octagonal well and the tomb of Ahmed Khan have been restored and they raise important questions. It is essential to know the history of octagonal structures in South India, their function in both Hindu and Islamic architecture, their relation to secular art in the context of other structures and objects found around the area as well the society and culture during the period. Hence it is essential to conduct interdisciplinary studies on the city and empire.

Hampi Research Project and Future Plans

Archaeologists in India have focused on pre-historic sites of early ancient period and early historic and medieval sites have received scant attention. Realizing this lacuna, the Union Minister for Education, Professor Nurul Hasan, also a noted historian, initiated a program of three National Projects in 1976. His aim was to expose the remains and pattern of three great medieval cities: Fatehpur Sikri in Uttara Pradesh, Champaner in Gujarat and Hampi (Vijayanagara) in Karnataka. The National Project of Hampi which is being carried out jointly by the Archaeological Survey of India and the State Directorate of Archaeology & Museums, Karnataka entails documentation, conservation, exposition, research and publications.

(a) Documentation of the material remains scattered over such a vast area requires the observant eye of architectural historians, epigraphists and others. Documentattion with the help of authentic maps, scientific surveys, air-photography has been undertaken by Dr. George Michell, an architect-art historian from London, and Prof. John M. Fritz, University of New Mexico, Albuquerque, in a limited area approved by the Archaeological Survey of India. This is very essential in view of robbery and vandalism of the remains.

(b) Exposition of remains of a large number of buildings, roads, platforms still under the debris, after the destruction of the city in c. 1565 C.E. is being carried out under the National Project.

(c) Conservation or monuments and all remains is an essential aspect as a large number of monuments are in a bad state of preservation. There are fifty six monuments which have been declared as monuments of national importance. Many of the national monuments, such as the Krishna and Vitthala temple complexes required major renovation. The masonry walls of the so-called Mint area, as well as fortification, gateways, and the bazaars required attention which the central ASI has undertaken.

(d) Architectural studies have not received the attention they deserve. Neither have authentic and accurate section, elevation and plans been published nor a detailed study of architectural groups, such as the royal enclosure, temple complexes, gateways and watch towers, been undertaken. In this context, it may be mentioned that Dr. George Michell, with his band of volunteer students of architecture both Indian and foreign has rendered a service by carrying out architectural studies at Vijayanagara for the past decade and half, and preparing accurate drawings of several major monuments in the Royal Center. Drs. Vasundhara and Pierre Filliozat of the French Institute, Pondicherry, have also made detailed architectural studies and drawings of the Vitthala complex in the city. Other studies that could contribute to our knowledge, would be on the irrigation system based on the existing hydraulic architecture as well as epigraphical and iconographical studies which will add to our knowledge of the social, political and religious aspects of the period.

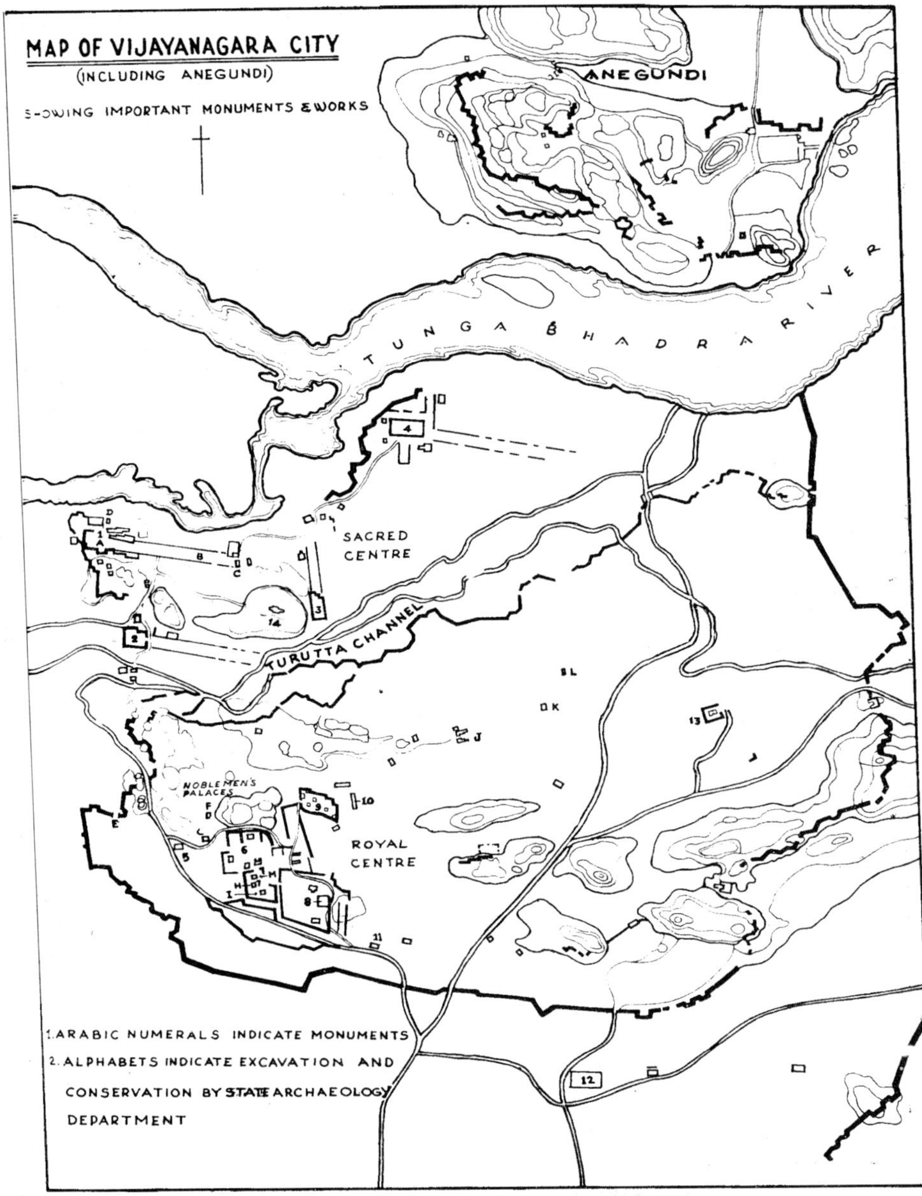

M.S. Nagaraja Rao: 1. Map of the city of Vijayanagara (Fig.)

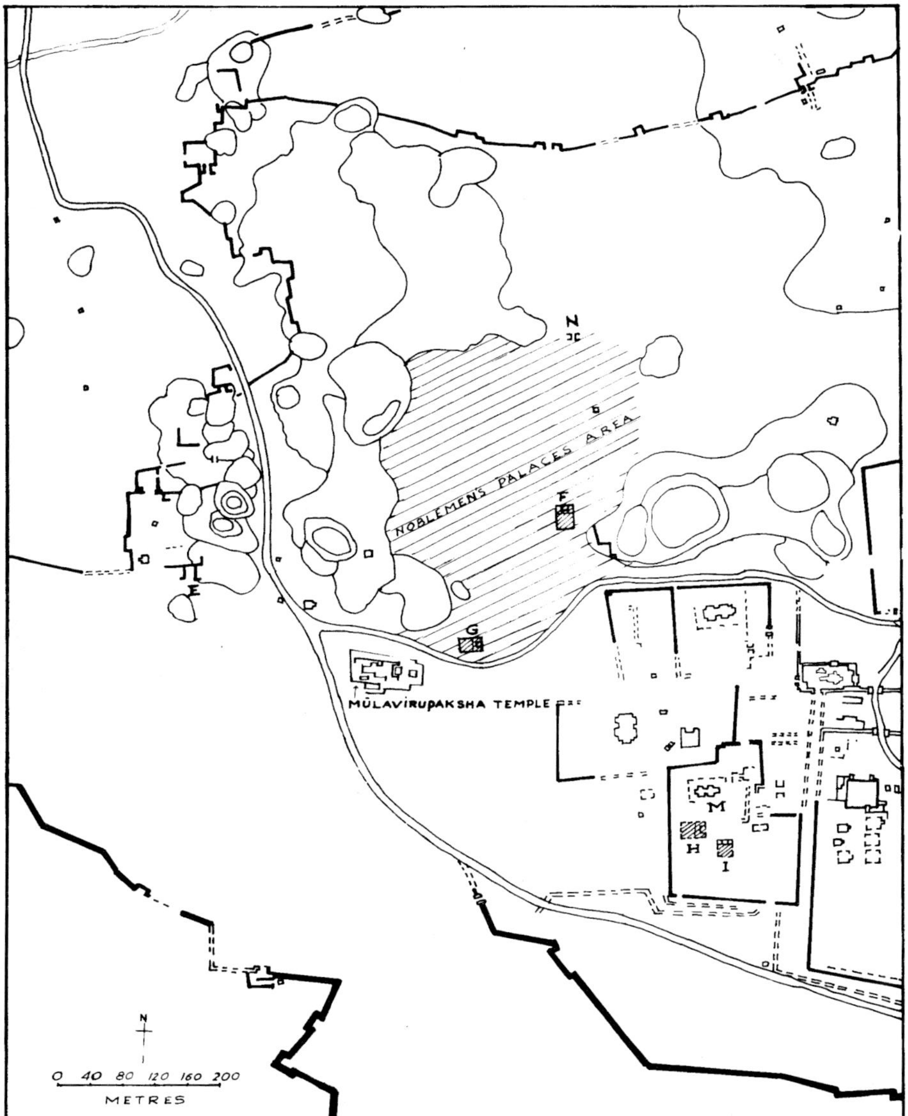

EXCAVATIONS BY THE DIRECTORATE OF ARCHAEOLOGY AND MUSEUMS, KARNATAKA.

M.S. Nagaraja Rao: 2. Site plan showing new excavations in the nobleman's palace (Fig.)

(e) Publications on those aspects mentioned above, is cruicial, in particular, a series of maps documenting all the features of archaeological and architectural interest.[9] The initial volumes include a detailed study of architectural, iconographica and epigraphical aspects of individual or group monuments in the city of Vijayanagara.[10] Concurrently, the reports of the progress of research (excavations, conservation etc.) every year is being published. The city of Vijayanagara is a vast area, and the National Project requires decades of continuous excavation, conservation and research. We have merely scratched the surface in unearthing and restoring the City of Victory.

Notes and References

1 Robert Sewell, A Forgotten Empire (Vijayanagar): The History of the Vijayanagar Empire. Beginings and Expansion A contribution to the Hisotry of of India (London: Swan Sonnesnschein & Co., 1900; reprint, New Delhi: Asian Educational Services, 1988), 88.

2 Robert sewell, op. cit. 73 ff ; John Dowson, comp. and ed., *History of India as* Told by its Own Historians. The Muhammedan Period. *Edited from the Posthumous Papers of Sir H. M. Elliot, 8 vols.* (London:Trubner and Co., 1872), *vol. 4: 88 ff.*

3 Ibid., 255 ff.

4 For the description by Conti see Edward Farley, *European Travellers in India* during the 15th, 16th and 17th Centuries (London: K. Paul, Trench, Trubner, 1909).

5 Ibid., pp. 118, 64 ff.

6 Elke Loschorn, Vijayanagar As Seen by European Visitors, in *Vijayanagara – City and Empire*, eds. A. L. Dallapiccola and S. Z. Lallemant, vol. 1 (Stuttgart: Franz Steiner Verlag Wiesbaden GMBH, 1985), 344-353.

7 John M. Fritz,George Michell and M.S. Nagaraja Rao, *Where Kings and Gods* Meet*:* The Royal Centre at Vijayanagara, India (Tucson: University of Arizona, Press, 1984), 9ff.

8 Fritz, Features and Layout of Vijayanagara: The Royal Centre, 240-256.

9 A beginning has been made by John Fritz and Geroge Michell in their work, Vijayanagara preliminary Map Series, 1982.

10 A monograph has been published by AIIS.

Figures

1. Map of the city of Vijayanagara
2. Site plan showing new excavations in the nobleman's palace
3. India in the sixteenth century
4. Royal and Sacred Centers, Vijayanagara

Descriptions of Plates

1. Gopura, Virupaksha temple, Vijayanagara
2. Excavations in Hampi bazaar, Vijayanagara
3. Mahanavami Dibba, Royal Center, Vijayanagara
4. Stepped tank near Mahanavami Dibba, Vijayanagara
5. Stepped tank, Royal Center, Vijayanagara

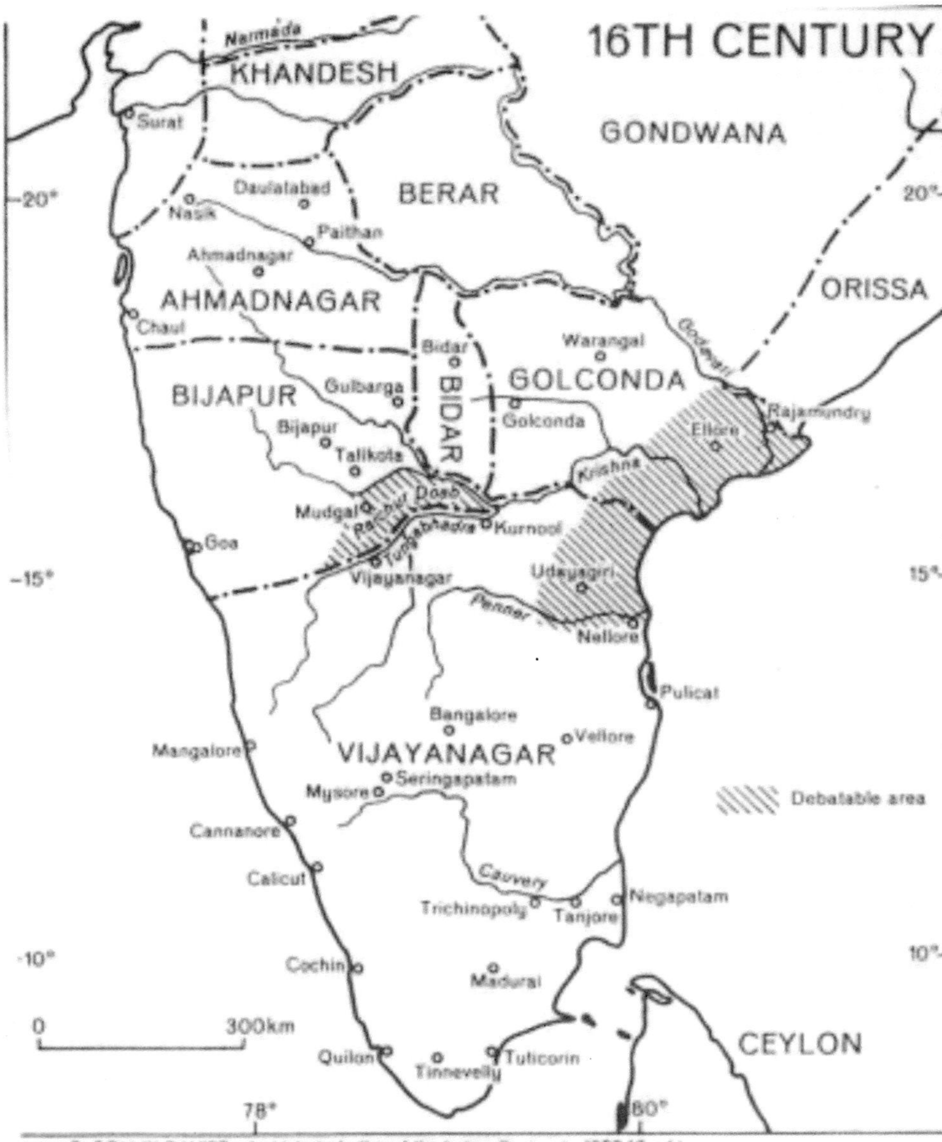

M.S. Nagaraja Rao: 3. India in the sixteenth century (Fig.)

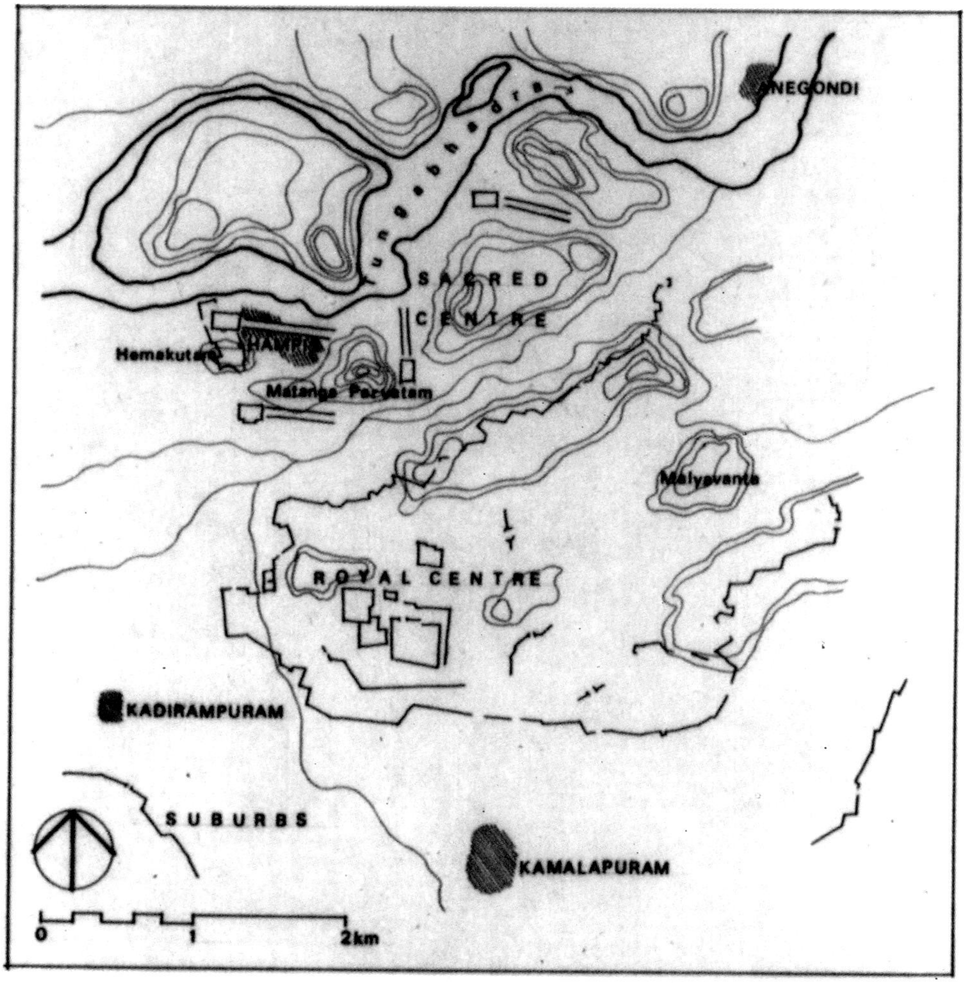

M.S. Nagaraja Rao: 4. Royal and Sacred Centers, Vijayanagara (Fig.)

M.S. Nagaraja Rao: 1. Gopura, Virupaksha temple, Vijayanagara

M.S. Nagaraja Rao: 2. Excavations in Hampi bazaar, Vijayanagara

M.S. Nagaraja Rao: 3. Mahanavamī Dibba, Royal Center, Vijayanagara

M.S. Nagaraja Rao: 4. Stepped tank near Mahanavami Dibba, Vijayanagara

M.S. Nagaraja Rao: 5. Stepped tank, Royal Center, Vijayanagara

3

Transformations in Religion and Art During the Vijayanagara Period

Choodamani Nandagopal

The complex interrelation between religion and art during the Vijayanagara period has not been given sufficient attention by scholars, although separate analysis of architecture, religious and secular sculpture have been undertaken. My goal is to explore this complex phenomenon in the light of royal and popular ideology of Hinduism and its workings in the environment of Vijayanagara temples. The changes and developments in religious ideas invariably transformed forms, styles, scale, content and meaning of the arts which effected social and cultural life of the people. Although it would not be possible to enumerate all aspects of transformation and the role of royal patronage, I hope to focus on the changes in religious faiths of the rulers and their patronage to religious arts, with special emphasis on evolution of new sculptural forms, and the literary arts. The influences of *bhakti* had a powerful influence on the religious developments and artistic changes during the period which manifested in the form of ritual, music and dance in temple cities that indirectly sustained cultural values and communities.

Protection of Religious Faiths

During the late thirteenth and early fourteenth centuries, the polity and social system in South India were dislodged to such an extent due to the onslaught of Mohammedan garrisons that it was a massive task to reconstruct a viable social system. The very foundation of the mighty Vijayanagara empire was built upon the aggressive spirit of preserving *dharma,* religion and culture. In fact the spirit of safeguarding the existing non-Islamic faith took the character and spirit of nationalism. This spirit infused new strength and enthusiasm to act in a constructive manner in the minds of the founders of the Vijayanagara empire. Their main concern was to preserve all that was non-Islamic and not to think about the multifarious minor differences of faiths existing within Hinduism. The major faiths and cults received royal patronage for construction of new temples, restoring the damaged ones, and additions to existing structures for the performance of elaborate rituals. Realizing the situation that only religious sentiments united all non-Islamic people, the rulers instilled confidence within all sects by showing reverence to sectarian gods and saints. Due to their continuous and sustained efforts to protect the people from Moslem invasions, so that they may follow the path of *dharma*, the rulers came to be known as *vaidika mārga samsthāpanāchārya, aparipālana, dharmasetunripāla, hindusuratrana,* protectors of *varnasramadharma*. The inscription in SII Vol.IX part II 441 refers to a slab set up in the Kundesvara Temple Condapura, and describes Devaraya II as *varnasrama dharmangala pratipalana.*[1] A copper plate inscription in the Triyambakehsvara temple belonging to the reign of Mallikarjuna corresponding to c. 1448 C.E. describes the king as the *hindurajya suratrana*[2] which referred to all those who followed non-Islamic faith. These *prasastis* in the inscriptions of the period specially indicate the need for an organized collective community and promotion of religious activities, and support to religious institutions. Folk cuts were revived by royal patronage and were officially supported. Through the cult of Veerabhadra, originating in Shaivism and the cult of Hanuman which arose from Vaishanavism, an aggressive martial zeal was cultivated. At a folk level the two cults invoked a heroic spirit. In addition, the deification of Kumara Rama (a folk hero) emerged as the third cult in this regard. The influence of *gramdevatas*, the rural tutelary deities such as Mari, Masani, Dyamavva and Durgavva were as important as the *Agama* traditions in the everyday cultural life of the people particularly in rural society.

It is possible to recognize three phases in the history of royal and religious patronage during the period. The first stage extends from c.1336 C.E. to c.1467C.E. when Virupaksha the last of the Sangama dynasty of kings began his rule. During this period of nearly one hundred years, the Vijayanagara rulers were followers of Shaivism, in particular the Kalamukha sect. The chief guru of the Kalamukhas was Kasivilasa Kriyasakti who was regarded as the incarnation of Shiva, and who was also their *kulaguru*, the family preceptor. He was a powerful religious personality who brought unity in troubled times. Soon, the faith was absorbed by the more democratic faith of Veerashaivism while the other sect of Shaivism known as Shaiva Siddhanta from Tamil Nadu was more influential in the establishment of Shaiva Agama traditions in temples. The Advaita philosopy proposed by Sri Adi Shankaracharya during the ninth century in South India flourished in the *matha* that he established at Shringeri and its teachers and saints had a tremendous influence on early Vijayanagara rulers.

However, we can observe a shift in patronage during the second period towards the Veerashaiva or Lingayat faith which was an off shoot of Shaivism and was promulgated by Basavanna in late twelfth century. It was a simple and broad doctrine, open to all the lower castes of society and which did not believe in elaborate rituals or worship in the temples. During this second phase, the *Dvaita* tradition of Vaishnavism also gained importance . The Madhva guru Sripadacharya was responsible for consoling Saluva Narasimha who had killed the Brahmins; but from that period onward Madhva saints began to be honored. It was during the period of king Virupaksha according to a Sanskrit Vaishnava text, *Prapannamrtam* by Anantacharya, that the king realized the greatness of *Ramayana* and embraced Vaishnavism. Among the Vasihnava saints and poets, Vyasaraya, the disciple of Sripadacharya was the pontiff who advised the rulers in political matters. His disciples Purandara and Kanaka spearheaded the Haridasa movement in South India. They granted large amounts of money, lands and ritual vessels to *mathas* such as those at

Shringeri, Udupi, Sosale, Ahobala, Sravanabelagola as well as Jangama *mathas*. Despite their personal affiliation the Tuluva rulers championed the cause of toleration and extended patronage and reverence to all the sects.

In turn, the religious pontiffs of Smarta, Madhva and Vaishnava *mathas* supported the Vijayanagara kings in their efforts to enhance the religious culture of Hinduism. Despite their ideological differences they exhibited a spirit of tolerance for each other and realized their role in establishing social harmony. Sage Vidyaranya and the Vedic commentator Sayana and his brother Madhava provided a strong support to the imperial rulers during the early and middle phases of the empire.

The third stage lasted from the reign of Sadashiva c.1543 C.E. to the fall of the Aravidu rulers till about c.1660 C.E. when the Srivaishnava sect gew in popularity. In fact, the Srivaishnava temple tradition was an overpowering influence in large parts of South India except among the Madhva and Smartha communities.

In regard to royal patronage to religious institutions, the kings supported all religious groups which is attested by numerous inscriptions. The Heddase grant of Marappa, a brother of Harihara I, mentions that god was pleased and caused king Sangama to be born in a great royal line for the protection of *dharma*.[3] A traditional account of the religious faiths known as four *samayas* or sects recognized Maheshvara or Shaiva, Vaishnava, Bauddha and Arhata or Jaina. Many inscriptions confirm that kings, queens and even the generals were addressed with titles such as c*hatussamaya-samudharana*, supporter of four faiths. It is learnt that during the period of Devaraya time even a mosque was built for the army consignment who were Muslims.

Temple devotion and its manifestations

The period was characterized by a vibrant expression of devotion to the gods, which led to the building of innumerable temples, small shrines, large *mandapas*, royal *gopuras*, images of Sanskritic and folk gods and goddesses, and those of saints as well. In almost every part of the empire, poets and *bhaktas* composed devotional songs on their *ishtadevata*, their personal god. The Sufi saints in northern India, the Nayanars and Alwars from Tamilnadu, the Dasas and Sharanas from Karnataka and the Acharyas, such as Annamacharya from Andhra Pradesh propogated the spirit of *bhakti* though religious poetry and music. They were joined by the wandering ascetics, the *jangamas* from the Veerashaiva sect, the Haridasas, the mendicants of Madhva sect and the progenitors of philosophy of Srivaishnava sect, with their will of surrender to the divine which appealed to the heart of the devotee especially in the precints of a temple. The manifestation of divinity took place through temple rituals which were, in fact, mediating procedures for establishing contact with the divine.

The revival of faith by saints, poets and temple priests was reflected in the carving of a variety of gods, both in the form of monolithic sculptures such as those of Kadalekalu Ganapati, Nandi at Lepakshi as well as small images in shrines such as *parivaradevata* shrines in the Virupaksha temple. Even mural paintings in Lepakshi and the Virupaksha temple in Hampi depict religious scenes, such as those of Girijakalyana, Nataraja, Krishna, Vishnu and Narasimha. Even the life of Tirthankaras, namely Rshabhadeva, Vardhamana and Neminatha are portrayed in a *sangita mandapa* at Tiruparutti-Kunram constructed by Irugappa, the minister of Bukkaraya II.

The evocation of a spirit of devotion in temples was enacted in music and dance, especially the *sharanagati* or the spirit of surrender. The Vijayanagara inscriptions also furnish evidences of grants made for supporting the *devadasis* or servants of god; they were the dancing girls in temples during the annual ritual festivals which were celebrated in the capital city. The Vijayanagara kings honored dancers, musicians and all artists with titles and gifts. King Harihara II is said to have made sixty seven types of offering to god Keshava in the Chennakeshava temple at Belur, dated c.1397 C.E. among which are the services of dance and music to be offered in the *mandapa*. An inscription belonging to the period of Krishnadevaraya on a pillar in Belagallu, Kurnool Taluk dated c. 1514 C.E. records that Basavaraja made a gift of a plot of land to the actor Nagayya, whose father had become famous in a dramatic performance. The gift was made in the presence of God Jalasingadeva for the merit of the king in appreciation of the drama; the hero and heroine is said to have received the best actor and best actress awards. Another inscription dated c.1552 C.E. during the reign of Sadashiva records the gift of the village Nankanahalli to god Vasanta Mallikarjuna of Devalapura made by Ramappa Nayaka. The village was to be enjoyed by the chief of *Nagasvara* players, and piper, son of Konnayya Ravula for playing on two *Nagasvaras* (pipes) and two drums in the temple; from which we can understand the importance accorded to religious music which was considered auspicious.

The Vijayanagara period also witnessed the flowering of written treatises on music and dance such as *Pampasthana Varanam* of Ratnakara Chandrasekhara (c.1430 C.E.), *Kalanidhi* of Chatura Kallinatha, the *Sangita Ratnakara* of Sarangnadeva, *Sangita Muktavali* of Devanabhatta and *Sangita Suryodaya* of Lakshminaraya Bhatta. The *dasasahitya* or the compositions of Haridasas and those of Vyasaraya and Purandaradasa are well known all over South India, as those who systematized Karnatic music. Purandaradasa is credited with 4,75,000 compositions which were passed on to generations through oral transmission. It laid a secure foundation on which the edifice of modern South Indian music has been built.

The sacred centers were made alive through different modes of worship, the rich lyrical compositions in different languages, ritual offerings to the divinities of food, clothes, jewelry, music and dance. The entire society was captivated by an atmosphere of religious devotion. By making the capital city of Vijayanagara vibrate with artistic forms and religious practices, the rulers created new traditions, standardized aesthetic traditions and expressions, which continued to flourish even after the downfall of the empire. It was a golden era when religious grandeur was expressed through the visual, performing and literary arts.

Notes and References

1 The *chaturvarnas* are *Brahmana, Kshatriya, Vyshya* and *Shudra*.

2 E.C.Vol.VI 99.

3 M.A.R., 1929, P.166

George Michell, *Architecture and Art of Southern India* (Cambridge University Press 1995).

S.Krishnaswami Aiyangar, *Vijayanagara: History and Legacy* (New Delhi: Aryan Book International, 2000).

Choodamani Nandagopal and Vatsala Iyengar, *Temple Jewellery* (Bangalore, Crafts Council of Karnataka, 1997).

Choodamani Nandagopal, *Dance and Music in Temple Architecture*(New Delhi: Agam Kala Prakashan New Delhi 1990).

Description of Plates

1. Golden *mukhakirita*,Virupaksha temple, Vijayanagara
2. Paintings, Kalyanamandapa,Virupaksha temple,Vijayanagara
3. Mandapa,Vitthala temple,Vijayanagara
4. Pillar,Vitthala temple,Vijayanagara

Choodamani Nandagopal: 1. Golden *mukhakirita*, Virupaksha temple, Vijayanagara

Choodamani Nandagopal: 2. Paintings, Kalyanamandapa, Virupaksha temple, Vijayanagara

Choodamani Nandagopal: 3. Mandapa, Vitthala temple, Vijayanagara

Choodamani Nandagopal: 4. Pillar, Vitthala temple, Vijayanagara

4

Temple Pillars: Their Evolution and Style Under Vijayanagara and its Successor

Anila Verghese

The objective of this paper is to explore the evolution of pillar-forms under the Vijayanagara empire and its successor states, the Nayaka kingdoms. During this period of cultural and artistic confluence, religious architecture in South India witnessed a tremendous increase in the scale of building activity as well as a reasonable unity of architectural and sculptural expression over a large area covering much of southern India from late fourteenth century to the early eighteenth century. During this period almost every temple was expanded by the addition of *mandapas* or columned halls; where the exuberant columns and piers were given special importance and grew to be the focus of the artist.

Vijayanagara was inspired by earlier architectural traditions of the Deccan and Tamil Nadu, which can be especially seen in its pillar forms. The most common pillar-type, adopted in the early-fifteenth century, was the five-part or the three-square block variety. The sixteenth century witnessed composite pillar types, observable in the form of a prancing *yali* and the column with attached collonettes. In addition, the horse-pillar and the pier with figural sculpture also make their appearance; although the popular pillar type with portrait-sculptures of the Nayaka period can be noticed in a nascent form. The column varieties that emerged in the capital city of Vijayanagara, the present-day Hampi, during the fifteenth and sixteenth centuries were soon disseminated over a wide area over which the Vijayanagara state exercised political and cultural hegemony. Following the disintegration of the empire, the artistic processes set in motion during the empire-period were not arrested. Rather, under some of its successor states, especially in the Tamil-zone, the composite column assumed new forms and greater significance in temple architecture and sculpture.

Introduction

The Vijayanagara kingdom was established in the mid-fourteenth century in the lower Deccan, with its capital in the city of Vijayanagara, the present-day Hampi, on the southern bank of the Tungabhadra River. From this capital city, the Vijayanagara rulers of three dynasties, namely Sangama, Saluva and Tuluva, ruled till c. 1565 C.E. over a vast empire, that extended over much of modern-day Karnataka and Andhra Pradesh and almost the whole of Tamil Nadu. Thereafter, till the middle of the seventeenth century, the Aravidu line of Vijayanagara sovereigns ruled from capitals that moved further south, first to Penugonda, then Chandragiri and finally Vellore. However, by the end of the sixteenth and early-seventeenth centuries. the processes of disintegration were at work and gradually many of the provincial governors, the Nayakas, asserted their independence, establishing independent kingdoms at Madurai, Thanjavur, Gingee, Vellore, Ikkeri and also at Mysore and Bangalore. Most of these kingdoms in turn declined and disappeared before the close of the seventeenth century, except in the case of the Madurai and Mysore kingdoms, which survived to the mid-eighteenth century.

For a long time, Vijayanagara art and architecture had been largely neglected; for they were considered to be inferior as compared to the earlier traditions of the south, whether the Pallava-Chola-Pandya artistic contributions of the Tamil zone or the Chalukya-Rashtrakuta-Hoysala traditions of the Deccan. Vijayanagara art and culture were often dismissed as decadent, as marking the end of the great art traditions of the southern India. It is only in more recent times that the Vijayanagara cultural contributions have been given their due importance and seen, not as marking the end of an era, but as the beginning of a new phase which had an impact on southern Indian cultural traditions till the end the eighteenth century.

Though the capital city of Vijayanagara lies in northern Karnataka, the Vijayanagara kingdom extended its sway over three major linguistic zones of peninsular India, namely Telugu, Kannada and Tamil. The artistic traditions that were in practice under Vijayanagara were elaborated by its successor states, especially the Nayaka kingdoms in Tamil Nadu. It may not be incorrect to say that the capital city proved to be a veritable cultural melting pot, where the following processes were at work: assimilation, synthesis, transformation, creation and dissemination.

Literary description of the religious architecture of the Vijayanagara and Nayaka periods refer to the increased scale of temple building activity and the unity of architectural and sculptural articulations. The enlargement of temple plan was in the form of additional *mandapas* (columned-halls), towering *gopuras* or gateways, and pillars. South Indian temples of the Vijayanagara era are built in a more or less uniform style that varies only slightly from one region of the empire to another; this trend continued to a large extent even under the Nayakas, with some regional variations. The various Vijayanagara temples in different sites, were virtually indistinguishable in their structural elements, motifs and decorations, but this imparted an overall unity to sacred sites throughout the empire. It may be argued that the addition of almost identical building elements was a royal means of manipulating the earlier sanctuaries and their religious cults. The scale of the pillared-halls and *gopuras*, especially the latter, soaring to ever increasing heights, proclaimed the resources and power of the state.[1] According to the architectural historian George Michell, style in Vijayanagara temple architecture, therefore, may be interpreted as a dramatic and highly visible expression of imperial ambition.[2]

Different stylistic processes are visible in the architecture and art of southern India during these centuries, which are not conceived as mutually exclusive traditions, but rather as overlapping and interacting movements. The first process looks backwards in time to past forms, which were imitated and then preserved through a conscious archaism. This revivalist tendency is best noted in the temple *vimāna* (the shrine and its antechambers), the most orthodox part of religious complexes, both ritually and artistically. The second process looks forward in time to new forms and types. This innovative tendency is most obvious in the temple *mandapas* and their piers as well as in the *gopuras*.[3] Although pre-Vijayanagara temples, in the Deccan tradition or in the Tamil style of temple building, had already their focus was on the *vimāna*. However, the creative trend of Vijayanagara temples, may be found in the use of the material granite which was a marked departure from the use of red sandstone by the Rashtrakutas in the Deccan, and the temple styles of the Rashtrakutas and the use of schist by the Later Chalukyas and Hoysalas. However, Vijayanagara temple-art was little influenced by these. Rather it was the local style that prevailed in the area in and around Hampi, which had an impact on the Vijayanagara temples of the fourteenth century.

The pre-Vijayanagara fourteenth century which are in the Deccan idiom, temples were of granite and fairly plain; their main focus was the *vimāna*, and the *mandapa* with its front porch, and had one or more small sanctuaries. The exterior walls of the *vimāna* are generally unadorned except for a horizontal band of scroll or geometric design (Pl. 1). Stepped pyramidal stone superstructures cap the *vimānas*.[4] Quite often, in front of the pyramidal superstructure there is a barrel-shaped projection, the *shukanasi*, built over the first antechamber. The *mandapas* have columned interiors and the hall and the porch may be provided with seating slabs.

However, the predominance of the Deccan style in Vijayanagara temple architecture, was short-lived. By the early fifteenth century the Tamil tradition, as it had developed under the Pallavas-Cholas-Pandyas/Later Cholas, had gained popularity in the city of Vijayanagara. In the Tamil style temples, the basement of the temple often consists of a double set of moldings. The walls of the shrines are rhythmically divided by pairs of pilasters into alternating projections and recesses; the projections have niches for sculptures, framed by split pilasters and shallow pediments; the recesses have isolated pilasters standing in pots decorated with bands and tassels (*kumbhapanjaras*). The superstructures of the *vimanas* are constructed of brick and plaster, as are the parapets that rise above the roofs of the attached *mandapas* and porches (Pl. 2). Another feature of the Tamil style, evident in the large temples of the middle and Later Chola styles, is the *gopura* gateway. The *gopura* comprises a stone basement, with a central passageway, over which rises a pyramidal brick and plaster tower, which is capped by a rectangular, barrel-shaped roof-form (Pl.3).[5] In the Tamil temples, especially under the Cholas where the focus of the artists was on exuberant sculptures that adorn the walls of the *vimana* and the niches set in its wall. The *mandapa*(s) in front of the *vimāna*, the pillared cloisters along the enclosure wall and even the *gopuras* are of much less interest as far as their architecture and sculpture are concerned. In contrast, when Vijayanagara borrowed the Tamil style, while the *vimāna* form was retained, the magnificent sculptures that adorned the niches of the *vimāna* exterior are not found. As for wall-sculptures on the *vimāna*, they are either non-existent or are given far less importance than sculptures in outlying parts of the temple, except in the earliest important example, namely the Ramachandra temple at Hampi-Vijayanagara. In the Vijayanagara and Nayaka styles of temple-art, the architect and sculptor gave maximum attention to the outer parts of the temple, especially to the pillars of the *mandapas* and to the *gopuras* of the temple.

Mandapas in Vijayanagara Temple Art

The number and variety of *mandapas* in Vijayanagara and Nayaka temples are much greater than in their Tamil prototypes. K.R. Srinivasan, the architectural historian, comments that the Vijayanagara temples are remarkable for the great size of their component structures, i.e. the *mandapas* and *gopuras*.[6] Percy Brown observes that much 'of the intricacy and rich beauty of the Vijayanagara type of temple was produced by the number and prominence of its pillars and piers, and the manner in which they were sculpted into the most complicated compositions, strange and manifold, so that each becomes a figurative drama in stone. Pavilions containing groups of columns form the principal part of the architectural scheme.[7] The varieties of pillared-pavilions no doubt increases greatly in Vijayanagara temple architecture. Besides the *mandapas* attached to the principal shrine and sub-shrines, there are the pillared-corridors along the enclosure walls, the hundred and thousand pillared-halls, the *kalyana-mandapas* (columned-hall in which the annual celebration of the wedding of the deity and his consort was enacted) and the *utsava-mandapas* (festival halls), the pavilions lining the temple-tank, the pavilion set in the center of the tank, and various other columned-halls both inside and outside the temple complex.[8] According to George Michell there must have been a symbolic basis for much of this imitative process: only an architecture that was firmly embedded in the past, it seems, could function as a suitable setting for devotional rites.[9]

Vijayanagara temple architecture of the late-fifteenth and sixteenth centuries and that of its successor states were predominantly of the Tamil style, especially in the form of the *vimana*. In the case of the latter, there seems to be a conscious archaism in employing the Chola or Pandya patterns of construction. In some of the Nayaka temple complexes there are even replicas of *vimānas* of the tenth or eleventh centuries. However, if revivalism and archaism dominated temple *vimānas* and their art, then innovation characterized other parts of the temple complex. The stylistic process that regulated *mandapas* and *gopuras* was directed towards the development of entirely new techniques, forms and images. A skilful handling of structural elements accompanies these architectural advances, for instance in the use of inverted T beams to span central open spaces, and the transformation by the sixteenth century load-bearing components into complex architectural and sculptural compositions. Piers in the mature phase of Vijayanagara temple architecture were adorned with multiple, three-dimensional colonettes clustered around the shafts, or were converted into large-scale, fully modeled figures and animals. Such virtuoso displays of sculptural skills are more conspicuous in halls and corridors than anywhere else within the religious complexes; so, too, is a newly fashionable imagery concentrating on royal and martial themes: kings and courtiers are portrayed as temple donors; armed warriors ride springing horses and mythical beasts.[10]

Evolution of the Temple Pillar under Vijayanagara

A number of pre-Vijayanagara temples have survived at Hampi-Vijayanagara, especially on Hemakuta hill and in and around the Manmatha tank to the north of the Virupaksha temple complex. The columns in these temples are fairly massive - each has a separate molded base and a shaft comprising two cubical blocks, at times with some reliefs carved on the four faces of each block, separated by a polygonal section. Above the two square blocks is the capital comprising a pot-shaped member, a disc and a *phalaka* (or plank-like part) with a convex base while the corbels are of the angled or beveled varieties (Pl. 4). This type of pillar continued into the early-Vijayanagara period, in temples built in the capital during the second half of the fourteenth century and even later (Pl. 5).

Although the above-mentioned variety is the dominant pillar type in the pre-Vijayanagara and early-Vijayanagara monuments at Hampi-Vijayanagara, there are other types that occur in this phase. Some pillars, which borrow from the Later Chalukya-Hoysala traditions, are of schist and are of the lathe-turned variety where the shaft of the column is incised with either horizontal or vertical flutings. Such columns are found in the sub-shrine dedicated to the goddess Bhuvaneshwari, within the Virupaksha temple complex, and along the Virupaksha temple chariot street along with the more traditional type of pre-Vijayanagara columns found at the site (Pl. 6). A much simpler variety of early pillar is found in the *mandapa* attached to the Durga-devi shrine to the north of the Virupaksha temple complex. This shrine, assigned on stylistic grounds to the ninth-tenth centuries, is believed to be the earliest surviving temple at Hampi. In the open columned-hall of this temple one finds very simple columns comprising two square blocks, separated by a round block and surmounted by a half-pot shaped member and angled corbels (Pl. 7).

Although the earlier types of columns, especially the two-block variety, did not entirely disappear from the repertoire of Vijayanagara temple art, it was soon replaced by the three-block variety of pillar, which rapidly became the standard pillar-type, not only in the capital city but also throughout the empire. In this pillar-type, the entire column is carved from a single granite block. The column comprises of a short molded base on which rests three blocks that are square in section, separated from each other by two polygonal blocks. The latter are either eight sided, or more commonly are sixteen-eight-sixteen sided. The five-part pillar-type, with three square blocks and two polygonal ones, has a decorative leaf or serpent-like projection, *nagabandham* on the top corners of the lowest block. In the more developed type, the middle square has small lotus buds at the top and bottom in each corner, while the top square has such buds at the bottom in each corner. There are relief carvings on each of the four sides of the three square blocks. The corbel that rests on the column is of the curved variety, ending in a flower or bud-like shape, and is thus known as the *pushpapodigai* corbel, which soon became the standard corbel-type in Vijayanagara and post-Vijayanagara temples of southern India.

Although a tremendous amount of work on the art, archaeology, religion of Hampi-Vijayanagara has been undertaken in the past twenty years, these questions about the origins of pillar-types have never been seriously addressed. George Michell, an authority on Vijayanagara architecture and the author of *The New Cambridge History of India I.6: Architecture and Art of Southern India-Vijayanagara and the Successor States* and the editor of the *Encyclopaedia of Indian Temple Architecture: South India, Dravidadesa, Later Phase, c. A.D. 1289-1798,*[11] shared with me his opinion that from the Vijayanagara point of view, pillars with triple blocks separated by polygonal sections are a local (Deccan) feature, as revealed in the Manmatha tank and Hemakuta hill shrines, and presumably in other simple Later Chalukya/ Hoysala period monuments. But columns decorated with figural and vegetal carvings may be traced right back to the Badami caves, so I think of it as a long-standing Deccan feature.[12] I was not fully convinced by this, for the Deccan variety of pillars was not of the three-block type. Hence, I looked to see whether the inspiration for such pillars lay in the Tamil traditions. I was surprised to note that such pillar types appeared in the *mukha-mandapa* of the Later Chola temple at Darasuram. The architectural historian Philip Wagoner confirmed my hypothesis, that Vijayanagara borrowed this pillar-type from the Late-Chola building tradition. He opined that this was a direct borrowing of the Later Chola *chitrakhanda* pillar type, as seen at sites like Chidambaram (in the cloisters of the goddess shrine and in the thousand-pillared hall) and at Darasuram in the *mukhamandapa* of the Airavateshvara temple and doubtless at other sites of the twelfth century.[13] Wagoner directed me to search in the *Encyclopaedia of Indian Temple Architecture: South India, Dravidadesa,* A perusal of this volume confirmed the existence of such pillars in the Late-Chola additions at Chidambaram and at the temple at Darasuram. In the latter, it was also clear that the corbel over such pillars was not of the beveled variety, as is typical in the Chola style, but was an incipient *pushpapodigai*.[14] Thus, the three-square block or the five-part pillar-type was one of many pillar forms that developed during the Chola period of temple construction. However, once Vijayanagara adopted it, it soon became the standard type of Vijayanagara temple pillar.

It is my hypothesis that the above pillar-type first appeared in the Ramachandra temple, constructed in the heart of the royal center of Vijayanagara city. This temple was the first major construction in the capital in the imported Tamil style and skilled artisans and sculptors had obviously worked on it. The strategic location of the temple, the remarkable quality of its architecture and sculpture and the royal imagery on its enclosure walls all indicate that it was a royal construction, datable to about c.1416 C.E., and constructed by Devaraya I (c.1406 C.E.–c. 1422 C.E.).[15] The Ramachandra temple is situated within a rectangular courtyard, the enclosure walls of which are adorned with extensive friezes of relief carvings. The entrance gateways on the north and east have columned verandahs, the columns being of the earlier Deccan type, comprising two sculpted cubical blocks and double capitals. The gateways do not have the brick and mortar superstructures that are typical of the Tamil-style *gopura*. Within the courtyard are the principal shrine and, to the north, a secondary shrine that is probably of a slightly later date, as well as two *mandapas*, one in the northeast and the other in the southwest corners of the courtyard. The principal shrine comprises a small square sanctuary, two antechambers and a square *rangamandapa*, with projecting porches on the east, north and south sides. At a later date an eight-pillared *mandapa* was added in front. Thus the architecture of the Ramachandra temple and its details embody the synthesis of the Tamil and Deccan features, with the former being more prominent. The southern elements are particularly noticeable on the exterior walls of the two shrines and in their brick and mortar superstructures. The column-type found within the *rangamandapa* and in the front eight-pillar *mandapa*, as well as in the peripheral *mandapas* is of the variety having the three square blocks, separated by polygonal sections, and *pushpapodigai* corbels. In contrast, the columns of the three porches and the two gateways are in the earlier Deccan style (Pl. 8). The influence of the latter style is also evident in the interior arrangement of the *rangamandapa* into nine squares and in the barrel-vault shaped projection from the superstructure of the main shrine. Thus, the Ramachandra temple is an innovatory work of architecture that anticipates the architectural creations of the Tuluva period.

My surmise that the new column-type appeared for the first time in the *rangamandapa* of the Ramachandra temple is based not only on the fact that in no dated temple prior to the construction of the Ramachandra temple is such a pillar-type to be noted, but also on the rather exploratory nature of the four principal pillars of this *rangamandapa*: they are of a black stone and so highly polished that even after the passage of so many centuries these pillars still shine (Pl. 9). Again, the sculptural themes found on the square blocks of these pillars are unique. For example, carved on the four pillars are reliefs of each of the twenty-four forms of Vishnu, the Chaturvimsati-murtis. In all of them Vishnu is seated and is flanked on either side by a consort goddess. In the entire repertoire of Vijayanagara sculpture, this is the only example of the twenty-four forms of Vishnu represented in this manner. There are a few other reliefs here, which to this day are not clearly identifiable. In regard to architectural motifs, in the *pushpapodigai* corbels of these pillars, the drooping bud at the tip is only present in a very nascent form. The pillars along the periphery of the same *mandapa* are of the more standard variety of the three-square block pillars. By the time, the eight-pillared *mandapa* was added in front of the main shrine (Pl.10), the Vijayanagara artisans seem to have perfected the art of carving this new type of pillar, which soon became the standard pillar-type.

It is interesting to find that, the Deccan style of temples and columns did not disappear from Vijayanagara city even after the construction of the Ramachandra temple. For example, the columns in the Parshvanatha Jaina temple, constructed in c.1426 C.E., are all of the earlier Deccan style. From the period of Devaraya II (c. 1426 C.E.–c.1444 C.E.), the last important Sangama ruler, there are two dated temples: the Chandramauleshvara and the Saumya-Someshvara. In their architectural plans, both are in the Tamil style. Yet, the four principal pillars in the *mandapa* of each are in the Deccan style, but with *pushpapodigai* corbels. Thus, the earlier pillar-type lingered on at the site for some decades after the construction of the Ramachandra temple. But, by the end of the fifteenth century it practically disappears, except for a few isolated examples.

It is difficult to state definitively why, from all the different types of pillars to be found in both the Deccan and the Tamil temple styles, this pillar-type was adopted. Probably, while importing the new Tamil style as it had developed under the Pallavas-Cholas-Pandyas/Later Cholas, this was the pillar-type that was the closest to what already existed in Vijayanagara architecture, namely the two-block variety, and hence was preferred among the number of varieties of pillars to be found in the Later Chola temple tradition, from which Vijayanagara borrowed heavily. Once it was adopted, it became very popular because it provided ample surface for the sculpture, since on each pillar there are twelve surfaces for relief carvings. For, as has been already noted, unlike the earlier traditions in both the Deccan and the Tamil zones, under Vijayanagara the maximum sculptures are found not on the main shrine or shrines, but on the peripheral parts of the temple, namely, the *mandapas* and *gopuras*. Not only did this pillar-type provide the maximum surface for relief carvings, but this type of pillar could also be mass-produced, as must have been necessary due to the tremendous expansion in temple construction that the Vijayanagara period witnessed, with either new temples being constructed or existing ones being enlarged with the addition of new courtyards, columned-halls and other structures. Once this type was adopted as the basic pillar form, an almost standard repertoire of sculptural themes came to be adopted for pillar-reliefs. The majority of pillars in these monuments are of this type and, of these, the vast majority are stereotypical and repetitive in nature. No doubt, there are some *mandapas* with pillars of exceptional quality, but the vast majority of temple pillars of the Vijayanagara-Nayaka period are mediocre in quality, with repetitions in motifs and sculptural themes. It is my surmise that such pillars were produced in bulk in workshops employing groups of stonecutters and sculptors.

The sixteenth century, under the Tuluvas, saw a tremendous expansion in temple constructional activities, especially in the capital city. Some of the existing temples were greatly enlarged; this was especially true of the main temple in the capital dedicated to Virupaksha, a form of Shiva, who had been adopted as the patron deity of the capital and the empire. Side by side, new temple complexes were constructed in the city of Vijayanagara. These include the Krishna, Tiruvengalanatha, Pattabhirama and Vitthala temple complexes. The period of about fifty years, before the destruction of the city in c.1565 C.E. after the disastrous defeat of the Vijayanagara forces in the battle of Talikota, was a period not only of expansion in constructional activity, but also of innovations in building techniques and styles, including the evolution of new pillar forms.

Large-scale temple construction was facilitated not only by royal patronage, but also by the overall standardization of building techniques. The grand temple complexes of this period have one or more courtyards, with towering *gopuras* allowing access through the enclosure walls. Besides the principal shrine, there are also subsidiary shrines and other structures within the inner courtyard. The *kalyanamandapas*, hundred-pillared halls, colonnades lining the inner side of the enclosure walls, the chariot-streets, which are also lined by colonnades, and elaborate temple tanks are integral features of the large temples of this phase. In the sixteenth-century temples, the Tamil temple tradition predominates. However, certain Deccan features survive, especially in the pattern of the enclosed *rangamandapa* with side porches. Occasionally the plain wall surfaces and the earlier pillar-type are also found. However, the superstructures of the temples are now invariably of brick and mortar, and the barrel-vault shaped projection from the superstructure (over the first antechamber) is no longer found.

With the enlargement in temple forms, there were many more columned structures within a large temple complex than had been found in temples built in the earlier centuries of Vijayanagara rule. While the three-block type of pillar remained as the standard pillar-type, new types appeared, many of which are offshoots or variants of the three-block variety. A number of the innovations in pillar-types can be attributed to Krishnadevaraya (c.1509 C.E.-c.1529 C.E.), the greatest of the Tuluva sovereigns. He was a prolific builder and the monuments attributed to him have new forms of pillars and also new types of temple-halls. The innovations in the layout of *mandapas* are seen in the *maharangamandapa* of the Virupaksha temple as well as in the hundred-pillared halls for music, dance and other forms of recitation and display, that occur in a number of temples in the capital.[16]

The *maharangamandapa* of the Virupaksha temple, or the long, front columned-hall of the main shrine (Pl. 11), was donated by Krishnadevaraya on the occasion of his coronation in c.1509 C.E. –c.1510 C.E. It has two side aisles and a four-pillar projection in front, which surround a spacious inner area, roofed with massive granite slabs. The monolithic columns of this hall are very ornate. The outer ones are of the three-block variety, but with a cluster of cutout colonettes, supported by crouching *yālis* (mythical monsters, of lion-like form) surrounding the main shaft. The pillars flanking the entrance steps, as well as those that line the inner open space are designed as shafts of the three-block variety from which emerge large-scale prancing *yālis* (some with the trunk of an elephant) with diminutive riders on their backs. The two pillars of the front projection, to the rear of the *yāli*-pillars, are of yet another type. These comprise a series of superimposed shrine facades, cut in shallow relief (Pl. 12). Thus, this hall has two types of composite pillars, namely the columns with colonettes and the columns with *yālis*. A third innovation is the pillar with superimposed facades. The location of these new types of pillars, as found in this hall, was to become normative. For *yāli*-type pillars only line open spaces in the temple-art of Vijayanagara and its successors (they are situated around inner open spaces or they face on to the outer open space in the temple courtyard). The pillars with clusters of colonettes, too, generally face open spaces. The pillar-type of the superimposed shrine facades is generally found lining entrance passageways, just behind the front row of pillars.

If we have to find the origins of the above pillar type, we have to look to the Late-Chola tradition for the answer. According to George Michell, the Vijayanagara artisans of the sixteenth century augmented the three-block variety of pillar, decorated with figural and vegetal carvings, by adding freely carved colonettes and rearing animals. Such colonettes and animals may both be considered a Tamil import since primitive versions of these may be seen in Late-Chola period temples, as at Darasuram.[17] If, in the later Pallava period temple pillars the prancing lions are attached to the pillar shaft, in some of the Later Chola temples one finds the squatting *yalis* forming the base of the pillar. For example, in the *mukha-mandapa* of the Darasuram temple, the eight outer pillars are supported by squatting *yalis* with their trunks curled up.[18] The same *mandapa* also has a pillar-type that can be considered the prototype of the Vijayanagara pillar of superimposed shrine facades.[19] Crispin Branfoot who corroborates the Tamil roots of the composite pillars, both of the colonette variety and the *yāli* type draws attention to the proto-composite pillars at thirteenth century Tamil temple sites: the Airavateshvara temple at Darasuram, the Nilagirishvara temple at Srirangam, the Bhojeshvara temple at Kannanur and the Kampahareshvara temple at Tribhuvanam.[20] Thus, it is certain that the three-square block type of pillar were borrowed from the Late-Chola tradition; in addition the new pillar types that appeared during the early sixteenth century, probably for the first time in the *maharangamandapa* of the Virupaksha temple, drew inspiration from the same tradition as well. But, while in the Tamil tradition all these forms appear occasionally and are not the only or even the most dominant pillar-types, once the three-square block type of pillar as well as the *yāli* and attached colonette type of composite pillars were adopted by Vijayanagara, they came to be standardized and to be adopted almost universally in temples throughout the empire. The positioning of the new pillar-types, that appeared for the first time in Vijayanagara temple-art in the early-sixteenth century, also follows the standard pattern. For example, in the *kalyana-mandapa* of the Vitthala temple, one finds masterpieces of carved pillars of the newly evolved types: the composite *yali* type and the colonette type, as well as the pillars with superimposed facades, all arranged in a manner very similar to the lay-out of pillars in the *marangamandapa* of the Virupaksha temple (Pl. 13).

The ingenuity of the Vijayanagara artisans did not stop with the above-mentioned pillar types. There are three more varieties - variants of the three-block pillar variety, which made an appearance in some of the Vijayanagara period monuments, but which were to be developed into major pillar-types only under the Nayakas. These are the columns with the martial theme of galloping or rearing horses; the columns with figure sculptures, often arranged in matching pairs; and the columns with portrait-sculptures of donors and patrons. The first two types definitely appear in the Vijayanagara repertoire. The third is only hinted at during this period; the true flowering of this type occurred a little later. While all the earlier-mentioned pillar-types, which became very popular in Vijayanagara temple architecture, were borrowed from Tamil prototypes, these three types were innovations of this period.

The pillars with the martial theme of rearing horses, which appear to be trampling on mythical monsters, with mounted riders, who are often armed, on their backs, is found at Hampi only in two monuments. The first is the entrance gateway to the Vitthala temple tank where two such pillars are extant (Pl. 14). The second is in a temple *mandapa* opening on to the Vitthala chariot street. The front row of pillars of this open hall has four detached and two engaged columns, all with fine reliefs. All the columns are of the composite variety and we find here three types of composite pillars: each of the two central pillars has a prancing horse attached to the shaft, the next two have attached rearing *yalis*, while the two in the corner have three attached colonettes each. The two pillars of the Vitthala temple gateway and the two in this temple are the only examples of the horse-pillar variety of columns at Hampi-Vijayanagara. Stylistically both the monuments, where such pillars are found, can be attributed to a fairly late phase of temple architecture in the city. Thus, this variety is an innovation started in Vijayanagara city, but flowering mainly outside the capital and in the period after c. 1565 C.E.

The composite pillar-type with large three-dimensional figures, cut in high relief, as developed during the period of the Nayakas, appears only in one monument in the capital city. These are generally arranged in matching pairs of figures, but are also found facing towards open spaces, either in the interior of *mandapas*, or at the front of the *mandapa*, opening on to the courtyard. At Hampi-Vijayanagara, such pillars are only found in the *mahamandapa* or the *uyyale-mandapa* (swing pavilion) of the Vitthala temple. This structure, built in c.1554 C.E. by Udayagiri Timmaraju of the Aravidu family, marks the climax of development of Vijayanagara temple architecture and sculpture. The *mandapa* is polygonal in plan and stands on a high plinth with intricately carved basement moldings (Pl. 15). Carved elephant and *yāli* balustrades flank the access steps on the east, north and south sides of this open, pillared hall. The virtuosity of the stonecutters and sculptors of this hall was primarily concentrated on the piers which are monolithic. The outer columns have groups of colonettes with slender fluted profiles clustered around the central pillar shafts. The piers in the middle of each side, flanking the entrance passage, also have, besides the attached colonnettes, fully modeled *yālis* in prancing poses. The interior columns create a large open central space as well as smaller open areas on the north and south sides. These inner piers depict combinations of clustered colonettes, rearing *yālis* and divine and human figures. The figure sculptures face on to the internal open spaces, or outwards on to the courtyard, as in the case of the figural composite pillar of Krishna dancing on the serpent Kaliya, located on the south side of the *mandapa*. In the north aisle, there are figures sculptures of divinities, such as of different forms of Narasimha. At the east end of the central aisle there are two pairs of figure sculptures of male musicians, playing on a variety of musical instruments

(Pl. 16). There must have also been a pair of female dancers, of whom one is still visible. In this part of the *mandapa* the ceiling has totally disappeared and the pillars, too, are mostly damaged. It is possible that there were other figure sculptures here that are no longer extant. Undoubtedly, the figural sculptures in this *mandapa* are among the earliest examples of this type of sculptures on pillars. However, at under a meter in height, the figures here are much smaller and less prominent than the examples of such sculpture that occur in Tamil Nadu a decade or two later.[21]

Pillars of the above-mentioned type, from which large figure sculptures (carved in high relief) stand out, are not found elsewhere at Hampi. However, that this type of pillar was being experimented upon and that it had been introduced into the Vijayanagara repertoire before c.1565 C.E. is clear when we look at another contemporary temple-site, namely, the Veerabhadra temple at Lepakshi. This site, where a cluster of early shrines were extant, was converted into a large temple complex in the mid-sixteenth century, by two powerful local officials during the reign-period of Achyutaraya (c.1529 C.E.–c.1542 C.E.). A later development in pillar-type is the column with portrait-sculptures of donors or devotees carved in high relief, depicted life-size or just a little smaller than life-size and occasionally even larger than life-size. These figures came to be represented in a conventional style: standing, with hands joined in adoration, in the *anjali-mudra*. This pillar-type does not make its appearance in Vijayanagara city nor, to the best of my knowledge, in any south Indian temple built prior to c.1565 C.E. However, the prototype of this variety is present at Hampi in a few monuments. A glance at these prototypes from a couple of dated monuments will give us some understanding of the evolution of this pillar-type.

Here, we are not referring to all portrait-sculptures that appear in temples (for there are many famous ones of this kind from the Vijayanagara period, for example the almost life-like metal statues of Krishnadevaraya and his queens at Tirupati) but only to portrait-sculptures on pillars. The first dated examples of portrait-sculptures of donors on pillars are probably from the Krishna temple. The temple was constructed by Krishnadevaraya, who, after his capture of the Udayagiri hill-fort from the ruler of Orissa, brought a statue of Balakrishna from Udayagiri and installed it in this magnificent and spacious temple complex that he built in his capital in c.1515 C.E. In the *mahamandapa* of this temple there is an unusual porch-like projection in the middle of the front, or eastern side, in which there are four pillars, with exquisite reliefs, of the three-square block variety. On the southeast pillar of this porch, on the west face (i.e. facing the sanctum) of the middle square, is the carving of a standing royal devotee with hands joined in adoration before Balakrishna (Pl.17). On the opposite northwest corner pillar, on the top square of the south face, is a similar noble personage depicted with hands joined, standing alongside a Shiva Linga. The prominent location of these two reliefs of standing royal devotees, with hands joined in adoration, hints at their special significance. In one scene he is shown worshipping the Virupaksha Linga, the tutelary deity of his capital and empire; in the other, he is paying his obeisance to the cult deity consecrated in this new temple that he had constructed.[22] The height from the floor-level of these reliefs is such that they would have been more or less at eye-level with any processional image of the god that would have been brought to this porch-like section of the *mandapa* for rituals on festive occasions. Although these are small pillar-reliefs cut in low relief and there is an image of a deity carved alongside the figure of the royal deity, in all other respects these figures of royal devotees are like the larger portrait-sculptures in high relief that are found in later south Indian temples, especially those of the Nayaka period in Tamil Nadu.

Another portrait sculpture can be found on a pillar is the one in the *mahamandapa* or *uyyale mandapa* of the Vitthala temple, dated c.1554 C.E., which was constructed by Udayagiri Timmaraju. On the south facade of the southeast corner pillar of this monument, facing outwards on to the courtyard of the temple, is a relief of a standing male devotee, with hands joined in adoration. It probably represents the patron, Udayagiri Timmaraju, himself. The height of this relief from ground level is such that when the processional image of Vitthala was taken around the temple on festival occasions, the relief of the patron would have been at eye-level with the image of the god.

Thus, during the Vijayanagara period there was a tremendous evolution in the temple pillars: from the pre and early-Vijayanagara pillar-types of the fourteenth century, to the three-square block type of pillar that was adopted in the fifteenth century, and then to the different varieties of the composite pillars of the sixteenth century. Before the end of this period, the pillar-type of the three square blocks with relief carvings, separated by two polygonal blocks, and capped by the *pushpapodigai* corbels, had become the standard pillar-type in south Indian temple architecture throughout the empire. The sixteenth century saw the introduction of composite pillars, in which the main shaft was generally of the three-block variety: the pillars with attached colonnettes or rearing *yālis* were adopted into the repertoire of Vijayanagara temple art early in the sixteenth century. Contemporary with these was the pillar comprising a series of superimposed shrine facades. The horse-pillar and the pillar with large-scale figure sculptures of divinities or humans came a little later; these types were not used on a wide scale during the Vijayanagara period. The composite pillar with portrait sculptures of devotees or donors did not develop fully during this phase; however, the prototype of this form was present in a very nascent form in Vijayanagara temple-art. Composite pillars are not just more decorative than the simple pillars; they have architectural significance as well. Being much more massive than the simple pillars, they allowed for greater distances to be spanned within temple complexes, supporting much longer beams, in higher and wider *mandapas*. They form a significant element in the architectural and sculptural development of south Indian temples from the early-sixteenth century onwards.

Pillar-types in Nayaka Temple Art

This paper does not go into depths into pillar-types in the Nayaka temples for two reasons. Firstly, unlike the case of the Vijayanagara temple pillar-types where little work has been done in tracing the influences that went into the different pillar-types and the evolution of the temple pillar forms from the fourteenth to the mid-sixteenth centuries, some study has been done on Nayaka temple pillars. I should particularly like to mention the pioneering work done by Crispin Branfoot[23] in analyzing Nayaka pillar-art, especially in Tamil Nadu. Secondly, so great was the wealth and variety of Nayaka art as it developed, with many common features and yet with regional variations, in the numerous successor states of Vijayanagara, that it would require a very detailed study. Hence, here my aim is to give a brief overview of how the Nayaka pillar-art took up from Vijayanagara and carried it to still further heights.

In the Nayaka period the *pushpapodigai* corbel is the standard type of corbel; the earlier angled or beveled varieties are quite insignificant in the temples of the Nayaka period. Now the curve of the bracket and the drooping bud at the end of the curved corbel become quite pronounced, adding to the grace of the pillars. What is also noticeable in the Nayaka period temples is that the columns, especially those facing into open spaces of *mandapas* or processional pathways, generally support a series of separately sculpted capital elements, stacked one upon another, including the *pushpapodigai* corbel and the seated *simha* (lion) above it and then another *pushpapodigai* corbel and ultimately the flat beams of the stone roof. These double and triple capital elements raise the height of the hall or the processional corridor that the pillars line. The double or triple capital is not an innovation of Nayaka art, for already in some of the later temples at Hampi-Vijayanagara they are to be found. One example, would be the central space of the *mahamandapa* of the Ramanuja temple, to the northeast of the Vitthala temple complex. However, while in Vijayanagara temples there are only isolated examples of rows of pillars with double or triple capitals, these becomes the standard format in the Nayaka temples.

During the Nayaka period, the simple column type, which had been standardized during the fifteenth-early sixteenth century under Vijayanagara, continued to be used side by side with composite pillars. Pillars of the standard three-square block variety with reliefs are found in their thousands: lining the temple cloisters inside enclosure walls, along processional pathways, within the huge hundred and thousand pillar halls and in the various halls and shrines within the numerous courtyards of a typical large Nayaka temple complex, for example those at Kumbhakonam, Madurai and so on.

However, it is the variety and size of the composite columns, with large-scale sculptures, that form the most striking feature of Nayaka architecture, especially in Tamil Nadu. These can be termed examples of architectural sculpture. These massive composite pillars permitted the construction of higher halls and corridors with wider open spaces than was typical till the last phase of Vijayanagara temple-art. Also, the sculptures of *yālis*, horses, figures and portraits are much more three-dimensional than they were during the Vijayanagara period. In many cases, these sculptures are only attached at one point to the shaft of the column. Thus, the composite pillars grew in size during this period, both vertically and forward.[24]

The *yāli* composite columns remained common throughout the whole of the Nayaka period and in almost every area of southern India during this period (mid-sixteenth to late seventeenth and even eighteenth centuries). On the whole, the *yāli* composite columns remain almost wholly unidirectional and frontal with little lateral spread. However, as compared to those of the earlier period, in Nayaka temples the *yālis* are much larger, growing both vertically and forward. Also, often the *yāli* composite pillar is composed of several animals, including a smaller *yāli* or an elephant on which the larger one stands (Pl. 18).[25]

Unlike the *yāli* composite column, which is found throughout the region, the columns with figural sculptures are found mainly in central and southern Tamil Nadu; this is a development of the Nayaka period temple art of this region from the mid-sixteenth century to the early or mid-eighteenth century. From the mid-sixteenth century in Tamil Nadu the figure sculptures on columns become a much larger part of the whole composite column and appear to be almost completely detached from the column support. The figures develop into lively fully three-dimensional sculptures bursting forth from the composite column. This is particularly true in the case of multi-armed deities, such as the dancing Shiva, while in the early examples of pillar-sculptures found at Vijayanagara and Lepakshi, the monolithic block of the column is clearly evident, in the later examples from Tamil Nadu the figures appear to be almost freed from the shaft; they avoid the rigid frontality of the earlier sculptures, adopting energetic, sinuous postures. Some of the best examples of columns with figure sculptures are in the Venkatachalapati temple at Krishnapuram (c. 1563-1578 C.E.), the Vatapatrashayi or Krishna temple at Srivilliputtur (c. 1572 C.E.) and the thousand-pillared *mandapa* of the Minakshi-Sundareshvara temple at Madurai. A detached *mandapa* in the Kallapiranswami temple at Srivaikuntam also has some fine examples of such sculptures (Pl. 19). Figural composite columns are generally placed in two main locations in Tamil temple complexes: along corridors or halls that surround and lead into the main shrine, and in detached festival *mandapas*. In the latter they feature on the exterior at the entrance or occasionally all round and more usually along the main interior aisle.[26] Another general pattern is that such sculptures usually appear in pairs: Kama and Rati, dancing Shiva and dancing Kali, Bhima and Purushamriga, Kuruvan (male gypsy) and Kuratti (female gypsy) and so on.

The horse-pillar also developed greatly during this period. Such of composite pillars are found more commonly in northern Andhra Pradesh and in northern and central Tamil Nadu; although occasionally found elsewhere, they are not so common in the Nayaka art of southern Tamil Nadu or in other parts of southern India. Besides the rearing or galloping horse with a rider armed with a sword or spear, a number of other figures also appear on the column either alongside or even underneath the horse and rider (Pl. 19). The best examples of such columns are in the Sheshagiri *mandapa* in the fourth courtyard of the Ranganatha temple at Srirangam and in the *kalyana-mandapa* of the Varadaraja temple at Kanchipuram.[27]

The composite pillar-type of colonettes attached to the main shaft also became more monumental. In the Nayaka phase, one occasionally finds monolithic columns with twenty or more colonettes sculpted fully in the round, encasing the core column to which they are attached only at the top and bottom. Such columns are prominent in the corners at the entrance to the thousand-pillar hall in the Minakshi-Sundareshvara temple at Madurai and at the entrance to the main shrine in the Nellaiyappar temple complex at Tirunelveli.

Another important variety of Nayaka pillar, especially in southern and central Tamil Nadu is the pillar with portraits of royal or noble donors or devotees, which as seen earlier, such type of pillars does not appear in their full form in Vijayanagara temple art. According to Crispin Branfoot, the Nayaka-period figural composite columns of kings or donors have a standard iconography: they are large-scale and often life-size, standing, rigidly frontal, with no suggestion of age or mood (Pl. 21). Individuality is suggested by their anatomy, facial details, dress and ornament. Headgear, for example, is the chief distinguishing feature of the ten Nayakas, with attendant figures, located in the Pudu-Mandapa at Madurai. More interesting than the identification of these numerous sculptures of royal or noble personages is the general location and function of these sculptures within a temple setting.

The large-scale stone figures on composite columns are consistently located along the major routes used by devotees going into the temple and deities coming out of the temple on procession, as well as along the interior aisles of festival *mandapas* in front of the platform where the deities are placed temporarily. Portrait sculptures are located at places where deities are normally absent but at certain times during the festivals, they are present. Thus an appreciation of a temple's festival function helps explain the location and iconography of portrait sculptures in the large temple complexes of Nayaka-period Tamilnadu, which are processional spaces for both devotees and deities.[28] Branfoot also points out that portrait-sculptures are uniformly in *anjali-mudra*, the gesture of greeting and devotion, and often appear above eye-level. This is explained by the fact that during festivals deities are carried through the temple on palanquins. The portrait sculptures are so placed as to greet the deities as they move through the temple on procession or rest in the *mandapas* temporarily during a festival.[29]

The above brief survey of pillar forms in Nayaka temple-art, particularly in Tamil Nadu, reveals its continuity with Vijayanagara art as well as its vibrancy and creativity. Regardless of the political and military weaknesses of many of the Nayaka states, this is one of the most prolific periods of temple construction in south Indian history.

Conclusion

Vijayanagara, borrowing from the earlier architectural traditions of the Deccan and Tamil Nadu, created pillar-forms, which while drawing inspiration from earlier types yet had uniquely Vijayanagaran characteristics. The column varieties that emerged in the capital city during the fifteenth and sixteenth centuries were soon disseminated over the wide area of southern India over which the Vijayanagara state exercised political and cultural hegemony. Following the disintegration of the Vijayanagara Empire, the artistic processes set in motion during the empire-period were not arrested; rather, under some of its successor states, especially in the Tamil zone, temple architecture and sculpture reached a peak of efflorescence. The standard three-square block pillar, produced in vast quantities, made possible the constructions of long processional colonnades, pillared cloisters and huge halls in the temple complexes of the late Vijayanagara and Nayaka periods. The different varieties of the more massive and complex composite pillars, with their greater load-bearing capacity, enabled the construction of halls and colonnades with wide interior spaces, often lined with columns of high sculptural quality.

The artistic levels of the pillars of the Vijayanagara and Nayaka periods vary greatly from very mediocre ones to superb sculptural masterpieces. It must be mentioned that only a few *mandapas* of the Vijayanagara-Nayaka temples have pillars that are all of uniformly high sculptural standards. Among such halls one can include the *maharangamandapa* of the Virupaksha temple and the *mahamandapa* and *kalyana-mandapa* of the Vitthala temple at Hampi-Vijayanagara, as well as the *kalyana-mandapas* of the Varadaraja temple at Kanchipuram and the Jalakanteshvara temple at Vellore from the Tamil zone. Many other *mandapas*, which are famous for some colonnades of superb quality, such as the thousand-pillared hall at Madurai and the Seshagiri *mandapa* at Srirangam, to mention just two, have some pillars of the most outstanding quality, especially those facing on to the courtyard or lining open spaces; but the rest of the pillars in these halls, especially those of the interior, are quite nondescript in nature.

This study of the evolution and variety of temple pillars under Vijayanagara and its successors, from the mid-fourteenth century to the end of the seventeenth and even early or mid-eighteenth centuries, proves that this period under Vijayanagara and its successors was one of tremendous cultural confluence and artistic creativity in South India. It witnessed the growth of an imperial temple-art, with regional variations and emphases, and with a richness and exuberance peculiarly its own.

Notes and References

George Michell, The *Vijayanagara Courtly Style: Incorporation and Synthesis in the Royal Architecture of Southern India* (New Delhi: Manohar Publications and the American Institute of Indian Studies, 1992), 65.

2 Ibid.

3 George Michell, *The New Cambridge History of India I.6: Architecture and Art of Southern India-Vijayanagara and the Successor States* (Cambridge: Cambridge University Press, 1995), 271.

4 Anila Verghese, The Evolution of Temple Architecture in Archaeology, *Art and Religion: New Perspectives on Vijayanagara* (New Delhi: Oxford University Press, 2000), 59.

5 Ibid.

6 K.R. Srinivasan, *Temples of South India* (New Delhi: National Book Trust, 1972), 168.

7 Percy Brown, *Indian Architecture (Hindu and Buddhist)*. 7th Reprint (Bombay: D.G.Taraporewala Sons and Co., 1976), 91.

8 Anila Verghese. Mandapas in Vijayanagara Temples, *Journal of the Asiatic Society of Bombay*, 73 (1998), 207-222.

9 Michell, *The New Cambridge History*, 272.

10 Ibid.

11 George Michell, op.cit.1995.; *Encyclopaedia of Indian Temple Architecture: South India, Dravidadesa, Later Phase, c. A.D. 1289-1798*, edited by George Michell and Coordinated by U.S. Moorti (New Delhi: American Institute of Indian Studies, 2001).

12 George Michell, personal email.

13 Philip Wagoner, personal email.

14 Michael Meister (editor) and M.A. Dhaky (co-editor), *Encyclopaedia of Indian Temple Architecture: South India, Dravidadesa, 200 BC - AD 1324* (New Delhi: American Institute of Indian Studies, 1983).

15 Anila Verghese, *Religious Traditions at Vijayanagara: As Revealed by its Monuments* (New Delhi: Manohar Publishers and the American Institute of Indian Studies, 1995), 48.

16 Anila Verghese, An Architectural Innovation of Krsnadevaraya, *Archaeology, Art and Religion: New Perspectives on Vijayanagara* (New Delhi: Oxford University Press, 2000), 208-221.

17 George Michell, personal email.

18 C. Sivaramamurti, *The Chola Temples: Thanjavur, Gangaikondcholapuram & Darasuram*, 4th Ed. (New Delhi: Archaeological Survey of India, 1984), 29.

19 Ibid., cover picture.

20 Crispin Branfoot, Expanding Form: The Architectural Sculpture of the South Indian Temple CA.1500-1700, *Artibus Asiae*, LXII, 2 (2002), 189-245.

21 Ibid., 194.

22 Anila Verghese, op. cit., 1995, 56.

23 Crispin Branfoot, op. cit., 2002., 189-245; Royal Portrait Sculpture in the South Indian Temple, *South Asian Studies*, 16 (2000), 11-36.

24 Crispin Branfoot, op. cit. 2002, 196.

25 Ibid., 196, 204.

26 Ibid., 196-203.

27 Ibid., 205.

28 Ibid., 241.

29 Ibid., 242 and Crispin Branfoot, op. cit., 2000, 25-27.

Branfoot, Crispin, Royal Portrait Sculpture in the South Indian Temple, *South Asian Studies*, 16 (2000), 11-36.

Branfoot, Crispin, Expanding Form: The Architectural Sculpture of the South Indian Temple CA.1500-1700, *Artibus Asiae*, LXII, 2 (2002): 189-45.

Brown, Percy, *Indian Architecture (Hindu and Buddhist)*. 7th Reprint. Bombay: D.G.Taraporewala Sons and Co., 1976.

Meister, Michael (editor) and Dhaky, M.A (co-editor), *Encyclopaedia of Indian Temple Architecture: South India, Dravidadesa, 200 BC - AD 1324*. New Delhi: American Institute of Indian Studies, 1983.

Michell, George, *The Vijayanagara Courtly Style: Incorporation and Synthesis in the Royal Architecture of Southern India*. New Delhi: Manohar Publications and the American Institute of Indian Studies, 1992.

Michell, George, *The New Cambridge History of India I.6: Architecture and Art of Southern India-Vijayanagara and the Successor States*. Cambridge: Cambridge University Press, 1995.

Michell, George (editor) and Moorti, U.S. (Co-ordinator), *Encyclopaedia of Indian Temple Architecture: South India, Dravidadesa, Later Phase, c. A.D. 1289-1798*. New Delhi: American Institute of Indian Studies, 2001.

Sivaramamurti, C., *The Chola Temples: Thanjavur, Gangaikondcholapuram & Darasuram*, Fourth Edition. New Delhi: Archaeological Survey of India, 1984.

Srinivasan, K.R., *Temples of South India*. New Delhi: National Book Trust, 1972.

Verghese, Anila, *Religious Traditions at Vijayanagara: As Revealed by its Monuments*. New Delhi: Manohar Publishers and the American Institute of Indian Studies, 1995.

Verghese, Anila, "Mandapas in Vijayanagara Temples", *Journal of the Asiatic Society of Bombay*, 73 (1998): 207-222.

Verghese, Anila, "The Evolution of Temple Architecture", *Archaeology, Art and Religion: New Perspectives on Vijayanagara*. New Delhi: Oxford University Press, 2000: 58-93.

Verghese, Anila, "An Architectural Innovation of Krsnadevaraya", *Archaeology, Art and Religion: New Perspectives on Vijayanagara*. New Delhi: Oxford University Press, 2000: 208-221.

Figures

(All the figures are courtesy the Vijayanagara Research Project. I thank Dr. John M. Fritz and Dr. George Michell, the Directors of the project, for their kind permission to use them in this paper).

1. Map of Vijayanagara City.
2. Three-square block pillar, *rangmandapa*, Ramachandra temple
3. Composite pillar, *marangamandapa*,Virupaksha temple
4. Composite *yali*-pillar, *marangamandapa*, Virupaksha temple
5. Pillars with shrines, *marangamandapa*, Virupaksha temple

Description of Plates

(All the photographs are by the author)

1. Pre-Vijayanagara temple, Hemakuta hill, Hampi
2. *Vimanas*, Ramachandra temple, Hampi
3. East *gopura*, Virupaksha temple, Hampi
4. Pillars, *mandapa*, pre-Vijayanagara, Hemakuta hill, Hampi
5. Pillars, *mandapa*, Parshvanatha temple, Hampi
6. Pre-Vijayanagara, Bhuvaneshwari shrine, Virupaksha temple, Hampi
7. Pre-Vijayanagara Durga-devi shrine, Hampi
8. East gateway, Ramachandra temple, Hampi
9. Pillar, *rangamandapa*, Ramachandra temple, Hampi
10. Eight-pillar front *mandapa*, Ramachandra temple, Hampi
11. *Maharangamandapa* of the Virupaksha temple, Hampi
12. Pillars with shrines, *maharangamandapa*, Virupaksha temple, Hampi
13. *Kalyana-mandapa* , Vitthala temple, Hampi
14. Horse-pillars, gateway,Vitthala temple tank, Hampi
15. The *mahamandapa* of the Vitthala temple, Hampi
16. Pillar, male musician, *mahamandapa*, Vitthala temple, Hampi

17. Pillar, royal devotee worshipping, Krishna temple, Hampi
18. *Yali* pillars, Vatapatrashayi temple, Srivilliputtur
19. *Mandapa*, Kallapiranswami temple, Srivaikuntam
20. Horse-pillars, *kalyana-mandapa*, Atmanatha temple, Avadaiyarkoyil
21. Pillars with royal donors, Rajagopalaswami temple, Mannarkoyil

1. **Hemakuta hill**
2. **Virupaksha temple**
3. **Ramachandra temple**
4. **Parshvanatha Jaina temple**
5. **Chandramauleshvara temple**
6. **Saumya-Someshvara temple**
7. **Krishna temple**
8. **Tiruvengalanatha temple**
9. **Pattabhirama temple**
10. **Vitthala temple**
11. **Ramanuja temple**

Anila Verghese: 1. Map of Vijayanagara City
(Fig.)

Anila Verghese: 2. Three-square block pillar, *rangmandapa*, Ramachandra temple (Fig.)

Anila Verghese: 3. Composite pillar, *marangamandapa*,Virupaksha temple (Fig.)

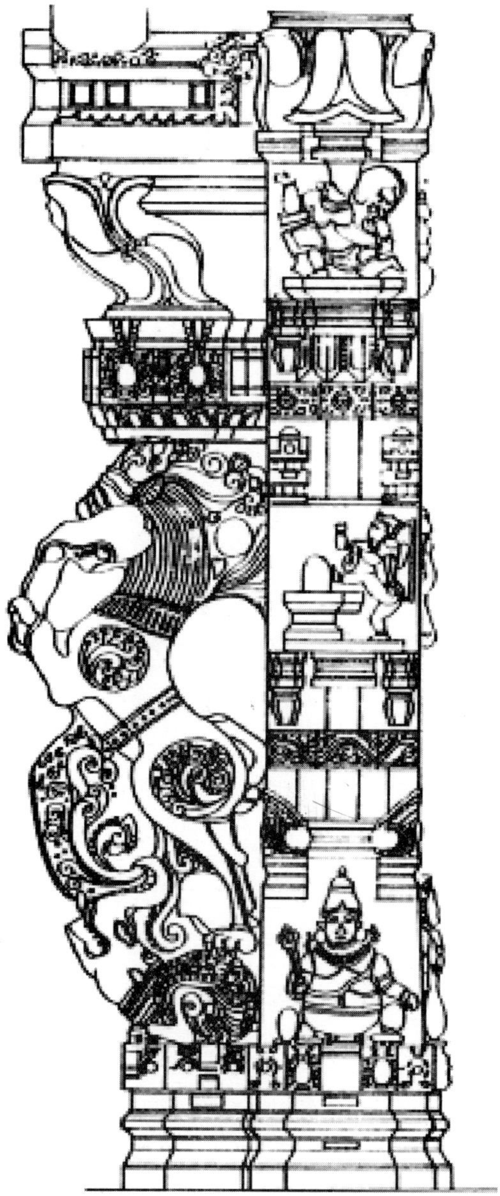

Anila Verghese: 4. Composite *yali*-pillar, *marangamandapa*, Virupaksha temple (Fig.)

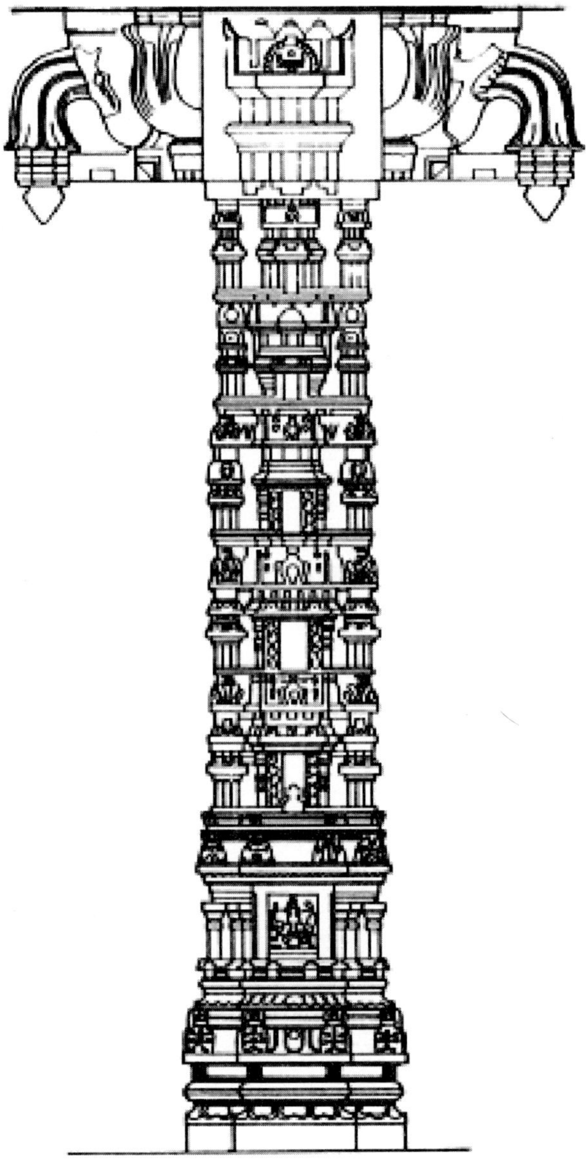

Anila Verghese: 5. Pillars with shrines, *marangamandapa*, Virupaksha temple (Fig.)

Anila Verghese: 1. Pre-Vijayanagara temple, Hemakuta hill, Hampi

Anila Verghese: 2. *Vimanas*, Ramachandra temple, Hampi

Anila Verghese: 3. East *gopura*, Virupaksha temple, Hampi

Anila Verghese: 4. Pillars, *mandapa*, pre-Vijayanagara, Hemakuta hill, Hampi

Anila Verghese: 5. Pillars, *mandapa*, Parshvanatha temple, Hampi

Anila Verghese: 6. Pre-Vijayanagara, Bhuvaneshwari shrine, Virupaksha temple, Hampi

Anila Verghese: 7. Pre-Vijayanagara Durga-devi shrine, Hampi

Anila Verghese: 8. East gateway, Ramachandra temple, Hampi

Anila Verghese: 9. Pillar, *rangamandapa*, Ramachandra temple, Hampi

Anila Verghese: 10. Eight-pillar front *mandapa*, Ramachandra temple, Hampi

Anila Verghese: 11. *Maharangamandapa* of the Virupaksha temple, Hampi

Anila Verghese: 12. Pillars with shrines, *maharangamandapa*, Virupaksha temple, Hampi

Anila Verghese: 13. *Kalyana-mandapa* , Vitthala temple, Hampi

Anila Verghese: 14. Horse-pillars, gateway, Vitthala temple tank, Hampi

Anila Verghese: 15. The *mahamandapa* of the Vitthala temple, Hampi

Anila Verghese: 16. Pillar, male musician, *mahamandapa*, Vitthala temple, Hampi

Anila Verghese: 17. Pillar, royal devotee worshipping, Krishna temple, Hampi

Anila Verghese: 18. *Yali* pillars, Vatapatrashayi temple, Srivilliputtur

Anila Verghese: 19. *Mandapa*, Kallapiranswami temple, Srivaikuntam

Anila Verghese: 20. Horse-pillars, *kalyana-mandapa*, Atmanatha temple, Avadaiyarkoyil

Anila Verghese: 21. Pillars with royal donors, Rajagopalaswami temple, Mannarkoyil

5

Temple Tourism in Karnataka: Some Late Chalukyan Temples

Gerard Foekema

Tourism in India has grown strongly in the last decade and the number of foreign and domestic visitors to places of architectural interest has reached a new level. In Karnataka alone, there are more than a thousand monuments belonging to a wide variety of periods and architectural styles, but the tourists are limited to only the Western Chalukyan clusters around Badami, the Hoysala ones around Mysore and Hassan, and the Vijayanagara ones around Hospet. One of the main reasons being the large number of monuments are in the neighborhood of urban areas than the isolated Late Chalukyan monuments in other parts of Karnataka. The Late Chalukyan temples are of special interest to an architectural historian as well as to the tourist. There are three temples in particular that I would like to focus on: the Mallikarjuna temple in Kuravatti, the Someshvara temple in Haralhalli, and the Mukteshvara temple in Chavudayyadanapura. The efflorescence of Karnataka temple architecture may be seen in these temples and they can be appreciated in the context of the Nagara and Dravida forms, of the role of articulations, motifs and sculptures which will convince the viewer and scholar of the need to approach this style with openness and appreciation.

The Late Chalukyan kings ruled northern Karnataka and Andhra Pradesh from their capital at Kalyana from c. 973 C.E. to c. 1189 C.E. Being the political successors of the Rashtrakutas they were great patrons of temple art and architecture. The Chalukyan king, Vikramaditya II was the patron of the famous poet Bilhana, author of *Chaurapanchasika*. The intellectual and cultural achievements of the period are reflected in the work of *Manasollasa*, the Sanskrit encyclopedia by Somesvara III, *Rupasiddhi* by Dayhapala who was the famous grammarian of the Shakatayan School, Ranna, the poet laureate at the court of Satyasraya, and the V*achana* literature initiated by Jedara Dasimayya, Basava, Allama, and Akkamahadevi. Other Kannada poets included Durgasimha, Nagavarma II, Chavundraya II, and Nagasena. In addition, was king Jagadekamalla who wrote *Sangīta Chudamani*. An epigraph of c. 1074 C.E. describes a great musician Mokari Baramayya who is described as Brahma of all arts. Royal gifts and endowments for the erection of sacred outstanding edifices enabled the construction of highly evolved temples in Ittagi, Dambal, Lakkundi, Gadag, Kuruvatti, Chudadanapur and Balligave.

The Architectural Style of the Temples

The Chalukyan temples of eleventh and twelfth centuries were built in a soft chlorite material which was a significant shift from the earlier red sandstone temples of the Early Chalukyas or those of the Rashtrakutas. It has often been remarked that the art of the Late Chalukyas has not received due attention despite about fifty surviving ones in Karnataka and Andhra Pradesh. Its architectural ramifications have been understood only in the context of a link between the traditions of Early Western Chalukyas and the Hoysalas.[1]

Many of the Late Chalukyan temples are considered a combination of the Northern, Nagara and the Southern, Dravida styles and therefore called Vesara. This has been called as the Deccan style although it is known to include the Vesara style as well.[2] However, according to Percy Brown, the temples were nearer to the southern variety than the northern.[3] Late Chalukyan temples are in fact, a combination of the two and every Chalukyan temple is very clearly either Nagara or Dravida; the differences are obvious. However the effect of the Dravida style is obvious, except for the Indo

Aryan *shikhara* and in some of its architectural ornamentation, although some are in independent style.

Late Chalukyan temples consist of the general arrangements of the Dravida temple, with a main building or central structure within an enclosure. The structure resolves itself into the cella *garbhagriha* or cella attached to a *sukhanasi* or vestibule, which connects with a pillared hall or *mandapa*. In front is often an open pillared pavilion or *mukhamanḍapa*. However, Late Chalukyan temples are distinct and are laid out in right angles, unlike the stellate plans of the Hoysalas. It is interesting to find that the entrance to the temples may be found on the side or the eastern side and may contain a portico or shrine. Regarding the treatment of the external walls, light is often introduced into the inner compartments by windows or perforated stone screens. Another additional feature of these temples is the projecting eave, with a curved section, which was not merely functional providing protection from sun and rain but also an artistic addition. All Hindu temple walls are normally provided with projections and recesses, and in Chalukya Nagara temples each projection of the walls is articulated as a heavy embedded pillar, and crowned (if the crowning survives) with a small curvilinear roof-tower. On the contrary, in Chalukya Dravida temples, each projection of the walls is framed with two thin posts and crowned with a small domed roof. These different walls give rise to different superstructures, but it is an error to think that the superstructure is the only difference between Nagara and Dravida temples. They are visually dissimilar and there are variations in architectural configurations, decorations, mass and volume which extends to the entire gamut of the temple, from the plinth to the crown. The walls of a Nagara temple look much more austere because references to architecture in wood are small in number. In Dravida temples they are large in number and entirely dominate the look of all of the elevation.

The temples have a pyramidical tower or *shimkhada*, but unlike the Early Western Chalukyan type with its defined stories, they are more closely molded. Light is often introduced by means of perforated screens. The pillars normally resemble the lathe turned Hoysala ones; some consist of a pilaster, around which occurs a pattern of leaves, mythical animals and figures. Another distinctive feature of a Chalukyan temple is the decorative doorway, both at the entrance and the one to the *garbhagriha* or sanctum.

The disposition of architectural decoration on the exterior wall surface is remarkable.[4] Here architectural decoration becomes a design element, which includes sculptural articulations: sculpture and architecture interact and produce an effect of intricacy and exuberance all at the same time. The temple walls are spaced by slender shafts of pilasters imparting a horizontal and vertical sense of continuous movement, in unending repetition. The decorative treatment of the wall surface with symbolic representations, gods, heroes, narrative stories, animals are ceaseless manifestations of architecture and cannot be separated from its background. If we were to compare the wall surface of a Late Chalukyan temple to that of a Hoysala temple, the latter appear over embellished while structural and spatial elements punctuate the Chalukyan wall surfaces. There is no dichotomy between the form of the structural members and the total box-like enclosure as the sculptural tendency in architecture operates strongly far beyond the confines of its actual measured dimensions. In this temple, it is not just the size of the temple but also forms that affect space; in fact the artist was sensitive to space emanation powers of volumes, thus awakening an emotional quality in the viewer and user. This total jewel box-like enclosure was the product of the operation of a sculptural tendency in architecture.

The Chalukyan artist was not merely an architect who approached space; the artist was a sculptor and a jeweler as well. The artist was trained in all arts: architecture, sculpture and jewelry and thus total artistic integration was possible. Forms are not restricted to their corporal limits, but overflow delicately and in abundance due to the skill of stone chiseling. The shapes, surfaces, planes and volumes that emanate affect space, which has now a quality of extreme richness, order and sacredness.

The Mallikarjuna-temple in the village of Kuravatti, on the right bank of the River Tungabhadra was built in the eleventh century and is one of the magnificent temples, in plan and surface decoration. One has to see them to experience the quality of refined visual delight. It certainly is worth a day of traveling, but the trip is the more rewarding because two other ornate temples, from the same period are standing nearby, on the other side of the river, in the villages Haralhalli and Chavudayyadanapura. Therefore, in the decades to come, Kuruvatti may appear on the tourist map. In one day, the visitor can see three beautiful old temples: Kuruvatti is about five kms. on the right bank of the river Tungabhadra near National Highway 13, Haralhalli is on the left bank of the river, only one km. downstream from the bridge and Chavudayyadanapura is also on the left bank, about 3 kilometers upstream from the bridge.

The Temple in Kuruvatti

The Mallikarjuna temple in Kuruvatti is dedicated to Shiva and was built in the second half of the eleventh century. Consisting of a shrine and of a closed hall with three entrances (two of them with porches), it is slightly larger than average, but in all other aspects it exhibits common features of a Late Chalukyan style. The large brick tower crowning the shrine has a clear outline while the projections and recesses contain surface decorations and a variety of motifs. Each projection, framed in the Dravida way with thin pilasters, is decorated with a miniature tower resting on two more of the same thin pilasters. Each recess is decorated with a smaller tower carried by one pilaster and canopied by a *makaratorana*. A few projections of the walls, however, are articulated and embedded with heavy pillars. This is common in Chalukya-Dravida temples; it is an element derived from Nagara temples but entirely integrated in the Dravida design. Two specially noteworthy features are the *toranas* or arched entrances with its massive lintel and the *sukhanasi*. These decorations are found time and again in the overwhelming majority of the temples of the period. The pattern formed by them is aesthetically appealing and well balanced. The embedded pillars are always found in the same places, never on a corner but next to a corner, and also on the wall connecting the shrine with the hall. Large sculptures of gods are absent in this scheme; they are not found on the walls but only inside large niches in the center of a wall. So in Kuruvatti: each side of the shrine has a niche, the sculptures found here are Bhairava (only his feet with sandals survive), a dancing Shiva and Ugranarasimha. As usual, each of the three niches has a miniature shrine above it canopied with a large *makaratorana*.

An uncommon element at Kuruvatti is the quality of the decorations; in particular are the miniature towers resting on two pilasters, as they consist of architectural elements only and nevertheless have a character of their own. The number of architectural elements is not very large and each of these elements is chiseled with love and care. As a consequence these Dravida towers are the most beautiful miniatures in existence. In many pretentious temples they have more *tālas* and are very crowded. Here they are simple and very carefully executed, and as a consequence they have a noble and solemn character. The miniature towers in the recesses of the walls are less beautiful, but the *makaratoranas* or archway above them are the most clear examples of the extraordinary quality of chiseling found here. These small *toranas* are found in large numbers in dozens of temples, but here they simply are the best: it is in the quality of these common decorations that the Kuruvatti temple is so outstanding.

Of course the temple has also decorations that are larger and not so repetitive. They are of the same superior quality and will not be overlooked easily. The three niches in the outer walls of the shrine have marvelous crownings; especially the *makaratoraṇa* above the southern niche is very successful due to the elaborate carvings. The three doorframes into the hall are very elaborate and very successful. The frontal entrance has three bracket-figures left that are extremely delicate and look like being made of metal. In addition, the hall has four unsurpassed pillars from where forms emanate ceaselessly. The entrance into the *antarāla* consists of a massive lintel on two free standing pillars while the great *torana* resting on two free-standing pillars, portrays from left to right Brahma, Shiva and Vishnu. The bracket figures at the upper part of the pillars are a bewildering multitude known for their delicate treatment, and sense of weightlessness as though they were made of lace. Here, even stone melts to create organic and ethereal forms.

The Temple in Haralhalli

The Someshvara temple in Haralhalli is a *trikana* temple with three shrines, which share a square hall, while the fourth side of the hall has the entrance into the temple. Built in c.1200 C.E. it is small but profusely decorated. Each shrine is complete with an original Dravida tower made of natural stone.

As usual in *trikanas*, the central shrine is more complicated in design than the lateral ones. Often the central shrine has five projections per side and the lateral ones have only three. Here, the lateral shrines have five projections per side, including two per side articulated as embedded pillars, but the central projection of each side is simpler and without a niche. Vertically, their number of *tālas* is one less than in the central shrine. In Dravida temples, the top of the walls of a shrine is repeated several times; the walls themselves form *tāla* number one, the repetitions are the *tālas* number two, three and so on. The lateral shrines here consist of three *tālas* and of a final crowning with a very large *kuta*-roof. The central shrine has four *tālas* and a crowning.

Seen from a distance this *trikana* is a marvel, especially because of the three complete Dravida towers. Walls and superstructures are profusely and beautifully decorated throughout. But seen from nearby and taken apart, many decorations are simple and some of them of little value. The latter especially holds for the miniature towers on pilasters decorating the walls; the difference from the temple at Kuruvatti could not be larger. But the miniatures as found here are more common, while Kuruvatti is the exception. Especially in Hoysala temples the miniatures can even be slovenly and odd. In Chalukyan temples they often suffer from too many *tālas*, as is the case here. Nevertheless the effect for the look of the temple as a whole is outstanding.

In the recesses of the walls the common narrow miniature towers with *toranas* are found, but with an interesting variation: small sculptures of gods and goddesses are added inside each *torana*. These sculptures are both simple and splendid, and the *toranas* themselves are of a comfortable elegance.

Each visitor will enjoy this miniature gallery of Hindu gods and their attendants. And also on the miniature roofs of the towers of the shrines many small depictions of gods can be found. The interior of the temple is elaborately decorated, more so than in Kuruvatti, but makes a less deep impression.

The Temple in Chavudayyadanapura

The Mukteshvara temple in Chavudayyadanapura is a small edifice consisting of a shrine and a closed hall with two entrances, and was built in the thirteenth century. While the entrance is frontal, the other entrance is lateral, making the plan asymmetrical. The shrine has a complete tower of natural stone and the state of conservation of the monument looks perfect. Moreover it is not located inside a slovenly village but inside a neat compound along the river, over which the view is very picturesque.

The shrine of the temple is small and has only three projections per side. As a consequence it has no projections articulated as embedded pillars; these are found only on the connection of the shrine with the hall and on the walls of the hall. The number of *tālas* of the shrine is three, and each *tāla* has only three miniature roofs per side; thus the architectural design is less crowded than in Haralhalli. But the decorations here are still more numerous, in fact they are more numerous than in any other Chalukyan temple. Only Hoysala temples can have the same amount of decoration. It is these decorations that give the temple the look of a jewel box, even more so than in any Hoysala temple, perhaps because the character of many decorations is not curly. Anyhow, the enchanting atmosphere of ornate Hoysala temples is found here as well.

The base and pedestal of the elevation consists of five horizontal layers and all five are decorated. The projections of the walls have crowded miniature towers without any eloquence, but they do not disturb the elegance of the other decorations. As in Haralhalli we here find *toranas* with small figures in their centers, and also here these *toranas* are very elegant and graceful. In Kuruvatti they are very different in character. A unique feature in Chavudayyadanapura is the curved eaves inserted as projections from the edges of the ceilings, which later becomes a regular feature on structures of this style.[5] Above the *chadya* (deep cornice) a row of enchantingly decorated miniature roofs crown the wall.

However it is important to note that the environment of a Late Chalukyan temple is far different than that of a Vijayanagara temple. The use of soft stone was highly suited for decorative carving, but the effect of the use of this stone was the reduction of the height of the temple which could not support a very lofty and heavy tower. The ideology of the Vijayanagara rulers necessitated building larger and more number of *maṇḍapas* for the performance of elaborate religious rituals. The three temples, the Malikarjuna temple in Kuravatti, Someshvara temple in Haralhalli and the Mukteshwara temple in Chavudayyadanapura, are known for their qualitative integration of the Nagara and Dravida forms, architectural decoration and exquisite workmanship. The Late Chalukyan architect was fundamentally concerned with the revitalization of the wall surface through small and large interwoven rhythmic forms. It was in the sculptural use of architectural elements on the walls, ceilings, and pillars that enchanted the user. The overpowering aesthetic environment of a Late Chalukyan temple is enthralling and the temples are worth a visit.

Notes and References

1 Susan Huntington, *The Art of Ancient India* (NY: Weatherhill, 1985), 543.

2 *Ibid.*, 540.

3 Percy Brown, *Indian Architecture: Buddhist and Hindu Periods* (Bombay: Taraporevala, 1971), 138 ff.

4 *Ibid.*, 144

5 B.K. Gururaja Rao, Chalukyan Influence on Hoysla Architecture, in *The Chalukyas of Kalyana* (Seminar Papers, Bangalore: The Mythic Society, 1983), 178-184.

Cousens, Henry, *The Chalukyan Architecture of the Kanarese Districts,* Archaeological Survey of India,1926. (Recently reprinted).

Dhaky, M.A., 1996. *Encyclopaedia of Indian Temple Architecture. South India. Upper Dravidadesa. Later Phase, A.D. 973-1326* Delhi:

American Institute of Indian Studies and Indira Gandhi National Centre for the Arts, 1996.

Filliozat, Vasundhara and Pierre-Sylvain Filliozat, *The Temple of Muktesvara at Caudadanapura. A little-known 12th-13th century temple in Dharwar District, Karnataka,* New Delhi: Indira Gandhi Centre for the Arts and Abhinav Publications, 1995.

Foekema, Gerard, *Calukya Architecture. Medieval temples of northern Karnataka built during the rule of the Calukya of Kalyana and thereafter, 1000-1300 AD.*, New Delhi: Munshiram Manoharlal, 2003.

Michell, George, *Blue Guide Southern India,* NY: A&C Black, London, and WW Norton, 1997.

Rea, Alexrander, *Chalukyan Architecture; Including Examples from the Ballàry District, Madras Presidency.* Archaeological Survey of India, 1896, recently reprinted.

Description of Plates

1. Tungabhadra river at Kuruvatti
2. North, Mallikarjuna-temple, Kuruvatti
3. Mallikarjuna-temple, Kuruvatti
4. Hal!, south, Mallikarjuna temple, Kuruvatti
5. Hall, south, Mallikarjuna temple, Kuruvatti
6. Shrine, south, Mallikarjuna temple, Kuruvatti
7. Entrance, east, Mallikarjuna temple, Kuruvatti
8. Interior, Mallikarjuna temple, Kuruvatti
9. Entrance, Mallikarjuna temple, Kuruvatti
10. Front view, Someshvara temple,Haralhalli
11. Shrine, south, Someshvara temple, Haralhalli
12. Central shrine, south, Someshvara temple, Haralhalli
13. Someshvara temple, Haralhalli
14. South-west, Mukteshvara-temple, Chavudayyadanapura
15. Mukteshvara temple, Chavudayyadanapura

Gerard Foekema: 1. Tungabhadra river at Kuruvatti

Gerard Foekema: 2. North, Mallikarjuna-temple, Kuruvatti

Gerard Foekema: 3. Mallikarjuna-temple, Kuruvatti

Gerard Foekema: 4. Hall, south, Mallikarjuna temple, Kuruvatti

Gerard Foekema: 5. Hall, south, Mallikarjuna temple, Kuruvatti

Gerard Foekema: 6. Shrine, south, Mallikarjuna temple, Kuruvatti

Gerard Foekema: 7. Entrance, east, Mallikarjuna temple, Kuruvatti

Gerard Foekema: 8. Interior, Mallikarjuna temple, Kuruvatti

Gerard Foekema: 9. Entrance, Mallikarjuna temple, Kuruvatti

Gerard Foekema: 10. Front view, Someshvara temple,Haralhalli

Gerard Foekema: 11. Shrine, south, Someshvara temple, Haralhalli

Gerard Foekema: 12. Central shrine, south, Someshvara temple, Haralhalli

Gerard Foekema: 13. Someshvara temple, Haralhalli

Gerard Foekema: 14. South-west, Mukteshvara-temple, Chavudayyadanapura

Gerard Foekema: 15. Mukteshvara temple, Chavudayyadanapura

6

The Politics of Royal Gifting at Vijayanagara

Nalini Rao

The ancient Indian practice of religious gifting or *dāna* has played a key role in the patronage of Indian temple architecture. Studies in South Indian polity and religion have drawn attention to Chola royal beneficence and the sustenance of gift economy which has initiated my examination of the implications of royal benevolence during the Vijayanagara period. I have attempted to understand the economic, political and sociological implications of royal charitable endeavors in the background of temple urbanism and network alliances. The visual arts in the capital city of Vijayanagara (Hampi) and the available historical evidences throw an interesting light on the transactional relationship between the donor and the ruler, authority and reciprocity and network alliances and Vijayanagara kingship.[1]

The popular practice of gift giving, *dāna* in a religious context has been embedded in the Indian psyche from ancient times. Gift giving was an apparently altruistic act which had immense *dharmic* and ideological value as it transferred merit to the giver. It was established as part of *rājadharma* and included individual gifting to *brāhmanas* and religious institutions. Even as early as the Sangama period (c.300 B.C.E. – c.300 C.E.) during the dominance of Cholas in Tiruchirapalli, Pandyas in Madurai and Cheras in Kerala, religious poetry was supported by royal patronage. The Pallava kings (c. 500 C.E – c.900 C.E) in Tondaimandalam proclaimed themselves as protectors of *dharma* and donated gifts lavishly to temples and *brāhmanas* at royal rituals from booty obtained from war thereby tying temple arts to political power. Gifting as an institutional practice of kingship gained importance when sacrificial kingship was replaced by the notion of *dāna*. Great gifts that were earlier considered as ritual dues and tied to the performances of the royal *rājasuya* and *ashvamedha* sacrifices during the consecration of kings now gained individual importance. According to Ronald Inden great gifts, *mahādānas* were performed as a replacement of the *srauta* sacrifices by the Rastrakuta king, Dantidurga, around c. 757 C.E.[2]

With the rise of the Cholas between c. 849 C.E. and c.1279 C.E., around the capital city of Tanjore, kings functioned as patrons of monumental temples which became the nucleus for the growth of South Indian urbanism. About 10,000 stone inscriptions engraved on the walls, pillars and even pavements of temples constitute a vast scholarly resource for a socio-religious understanding of gifting. By the time of the Cholas, the great gift ceremony became a "principal ritual modality of kingly beneficence as well as a sign of overlordship and independence."[3] The Rashtrakuta kings performed large gifting ceremonies as *mahādānas*,[4] and by fourteenth century, liberal gifts to temples and *brāhmanas* had become an established mode of *rājadharma*.

During the Vijayanagara period, construction of temples was a forceful precedent for the kings' re-establishment of Hinduism. The kings of Sangama, Suluva, Tuluva and Aravidu dynasties were responsible for the restoration of innumerable temples, construction of new *maṇḍapas*, and elaboration of temple organizations in many temple towns and cities.[5] Innumerable inscriptions in Karnataka, Tamil Nadu and Andhra Pradesh provide substantial evidence of a large variety of gifts, their purpose as well as the occasion. Although all the religious gifts may be considered as devotional in purpose, the gifts had various other functions besides the king achieving spiritual benefit for the worshippers.[6] Gifts were made for the construction of large and small temples, for worship and maintenance of rituals; they ranged from small articles for ritual worship to large sums of gold and money to tracts of land. Gifts were made on every important occasion, such as the founding of a dynasty, coronation or eclipse, or commemorative of victories or coronations. Two records in the Virupaksha temple refer to the coronation of Krishnadevaraya and few additions to the temple of Virupaksha to commemorate the event.[7] The *gopura* of the Vitthalaswami temple was built in c. 1513 C.E. by Krishnadevaraya and his two queens after the capture of Udayagiri and the king is said to have visited Shrishailam and Ahobalam, where he made donations and benefited the temples. During the period under review, there was a tremendous increase in the number of large gifts, *mahādānas* which were both one time donations as well as annual gifts.[8]

Before I begin the discussion about the devotional and symbolic value of royal benevolence, I will look at the materiality of royal charity, its role and objectives within a network system. In South India, temples had always played a key role in the process of urbanization and in the development of markets especially during the Chola period. They continued to be the nucleus for the growth of a vibrant economic system which functioned within a broader built environment in the fourteenth century.[9] Gifting initiated and aided a pattern of exchange that sustained agrirculture, market and industries.

The Temple and Market

The Vijayanagara king granted large land grants to temples on every important occasion; he donated tax free lands and sometimes assigned them certain taxes that were payable to the court. In addition, nobles and merchants made gifts of villages, *dévadāna* with its lands to the temple, and the donor renounced all rights including that of levying taxes.[10] As a consequence, the temples as landlords cultivated lands, or leased lands to tenant farmers,[11] acted as treasuries to agriculturists, rehabilited villages, encouraged reclamation of waste lands, extended cultivation and constructed irrigation facilities in order to increase resources and income of the temples, thereby expanding the agricultural base of the capital.[12] The larger Vijayanagara temples, such as those around the capital city, functioned as both promoters of agriculture as well as consumers of goods.

With the multiple functions of worship, ritual celebration, teaching and feeding, the temples utilized a variety of food articles, including coconut, rice, turmeric, incense, leaves, flowers, lights, butter, salt, pepper, arecanut, betel, oil, mustard, sugar, plantains, leaves, flowers, lamps, butter, salt, pepper, mustard, pulses, sugar, bananas, firewood, cotton clothing, as well as articles from foreign markets, musk, camphor, saffron. Indirectly, the demand promoted industries such as cotton, jewelry and stone workers. The important industries that grew around Vijayanagara temple towns were those of artisans, weavers, oil pressers, ceramic vessels, textiles, jewelry, armor, weapons, stone carvers, leather workers, barbers, potters and washers. The temples even constructed the road system for effective transportation of food and distribution of goods around the capital, thereby playing a significant role in the urban landscape in the temple cities or *puras* in the capital city of Vijayanagara.

The King, Temple and Guild

As a religious institution, the temple was obliged to perform a large variety of rituals, which had increased substantially. This required the employment of ritual specialists, priests, managers, accountants, watchmen, storekeepers, drummers, singers, conch-blowers, parasol- bearers, gardeners, dancing girls, musicians, and *brāhmanas* to recite *mantras* or chants. Temple staff was paid either in cash or kind and sometimes with land which could not be sold or mortgaged. Although the temple was a landholder, promoter of industries and employer its administration came under the growing control of royalty which developed its network of temple controls through endowments to *brāhmanas* who functioned through temples and did not act as independent landlords.[13] The temple economy at Vijayanagara and in many temple cities in the empire, was tied to the charities of the king and sometimes acted as his agent. Temples acted as tax collectors, and taxed the industries and shops located in the market just outside their enclosures at Hampi. They taxed *amgadi* or shops, *magga* or weaving looms, *pimjanigara* or comber of cotton, *agasaru* or washerman, *talavarike* or police, *hulubamni* or hay collector, *uppinamole* or salt pan and crops and even the ferry service across the Tunga river.[14] Being central to the production and exchange system, it is not surprising to find the temple cities dominating the *rathāpathis* or market streets at Vijayanagara, the hinterland and villages outside its walls, while the security for all these interlinked organizations was provided by the king.[15]

The architectural assemblage of the temple cities of Krishnapura, Vitthalapura, Virupakshapura and Tiruvengalanathapura, were agro-urban creations. These complexes were built from large grants made by kings and nobles. Distinguished by a large enclosure within which were tanks, wells, schools, they were entered through a towered gate and approached by a long colonnade street which functioned as a market or bazaar for the exchange of goods (Pl. 1). In these markets along the chariot streets, were sold gold, rubies, pearls, diamonds openly in the bazaars.[16] Each temple complex was surrounded by an agricultural hinterland, residences, craft industries, markets and water facilities which were strongly tied to local political economy.

Vijayanagara was, in fact, a conglomeration of local markets, called *nagara*; it was a *nagara* or city in the sense of a commercial city, distinct from its agricultural communities called *ur* which was dominated by non-*brāhmanas* and a *brahmadéya* by *brāhmanas*. Vijayanagara which had[17] a vast population[18] functioned as a spot of redistribution, allowing goods from external to local cluster of villages, and local goods to a wider network of commercial exchange-including the coastal market through itinerant traders, especially to trade with the Portuguese for war horses.

It may be appropriate to mention here that the term *nagara* was also a designation used for towns whenever land was donated to a *pura*. The Vijayanagara kings renamed the towns after royalty, which was not unknown during Chola times. Vijayapura was changed to Vijaya Virupaksha Hosapattana by Vira Virupaksha Ballala[19] and later to Vijaya Virupakshpattana by Ballala IV[20] and finally to Vijayanagara. The renaming of towns after royal personages was marked during the period of Krishnadevaraya who named Tirumaladevipattana after his chief queen, Tirumaladevi and Nagalapura after the queen mother, Nagaladevi. The town of Achyutapura and Varadajammanapattana were constructed and named after the king and that of his principal wife, Varadajamma. The intention behind the renaming appears to be the integration of the local area into the Vijayanagara political system. In addition, the renaming meant subjecting the *nagara* and its hinterlands to certain amount of royal regulation as well as transfer of power from the local agricultural institution to a commercial institution, the *nagara*. The *nagara* was dominated by merchants who invested their surplus in a market and even administered the markets in the capital city.

The *nagara* elite was the commercial elite, including traders and merchants. The latter who played an important role in the commercial life of the city contributed significantly to the brisk volume of trade.[21] They were organized in guilds, known by different names, such as *ubhaya nana desis, nanadesis, virabanajigas, vaishyas, settis, ayyavole, ayyavole salumulas of the fifty six countries*.[22] The guilds regulated and protected trade, carried on trade individually and collectively, and also organized weekly markets or fairs called *santhes*,[23] collected mercantile tolls at these fairs as well as the market taxes. Merchant guilds, such as the Five Hundred Swamis of Aiyyavole, (who dominated the trade of almost the whole of South India and were reputed for their benevolence in building temples) and the Salu Mule Banjigas collected taxes from community leaders and transferred them to the Vijayanagara representatives of kings.[24] The kings who stood to benefit from their wealth, were concerned over their control and protection of temple towns as trading centers whether they were on the west coast or in all market towns and especially those at Vijayanagara and thus constructed fortification walls around the market towns and settlement areas. The markets also provided a link between the city dwellers and those outside the city for exchange of products. They were links for inter-regional trade with other towns such as Hastinavati, Dorasamudra, Gutti, Pinugonda, Udayagiri, Changdragiri.[25] This link was of importance and had its roots in the genesis of the city itself.[26] These interconnected markets were linked as much to the temples, industries and communities. Hence it is not surprising to find gates, and routes linking the markets and temples in the city of Vijayangara where markets, communities and temples were all incorporated within the enclosure walls under the broad protection of royalty. The wealth of the temples cities (with their bazaars) was protected and demarcated by a circuit of fortification walls for security as they owed their wealth to royal benefaction by kings. Gates and roads linked the stable features of the landscape, commercial, religious and political which were organized in an inter-exchange through which economic redistribution was possible.

The preceding discussion provides a partial explanation of a variety of network alliances between three more or less independent and interdependent forms, the king, temple and the guild. The main actor was the king who through royal gifting and patronage, generated unique path dependences; the temple developed strong ties of association, and the guild adapted itself to the complex sociological environment. The advantages of co-operation and reciprocity were based upon the nature of power relations and bargaining positions. Although at Vijayanagara the architect of decision making was the king with his powers of gifting, what mattered more was that the reciprocity of relations was embedded in the social and cultural practices. Conventions were set up which defined the enduring qualities of networks – their stability, degree of coherence and efficiency. In summary, the nature of interaction between network alliances, the vitality of patterns of interaction as well as the institutional form, shape and character of the three main networks – king, temple and guild – influenced interdependent governance and the sustenance of a redistributive gift economy.

Artistic Evidences

Although the use value of gifting was substantially immense for the economic sustenance of the city, the extent of economic dependence upon royal land and money endowments is difficult to understand in the absence of detailed records. However, the sociological implications of royal gifting may be conjectured by artistic evidences. Two unique royal images are found at Vijayanagara which offer a new insight about the function and role of gifting in the history of South Indian art. One of them is a scene of royal gifting found in the courtyard of the Tiruvengalanatha temple in

Tiruvengalanathapura (Pl. 2). In a small shrine on the north side of the temple, but within the enclosure, is a *maṇḍapa* with four pillars. On each pillar is a portrait of a king facing the entrance and who is highly visible from the courtyard (Pl.3). The identification of the portrait as that of a king can be established with reasonable certainty, through the criteria of *lakshanas* or iconographical marks of royalty- cap, earrings and drapery. More significant is the architectural context as the temple was built by Achyutaraya; as well as on an idiosyncratic feature, his stout physiognomy.[27] On the pillar at the back, is a portrait image which depicts a figure wearing an upper and lower garment in a gesture of gifing: with the thumb and first finger joined and the other three extended (Pls. 4a, 4b). On his right side is a young *brāhmana* boy: his head is shaven and he has a small pony tail and his arms are extended as though he is receiving the gift. From the inscriptional record, we can gather that Achyutaraya made numerous donations to *brāhmanas* and priests with gifts of gold, village and lands. There are about nine inscriptional records which praise the gifts of Achyutaraya and he was known for his generosity and magnanimity.

Achyutaraya made numerous donations to temples, *brāhmana* and poets,[28] with gifts of gold, villages and lands. There are altogether nine inscriptional records at Vijayanagara which praise the gifts of Achyutaraya. Achyutaraya visited Kanchipuram in c. 1532 C.E. and had himself weighed against gold. Another record of Achyutaraya may is in the Vitthala temple which refers to the gift of the golden mountain *suvarnameru* by Acyhutaraya in c.1533 CE.[29] However, it is interesting to know whether the above mentioned gift giving scene depicts a specific gift made by the king orwhether it represents a generic scene. Among the nine inscriptions of Achyutaraya, seven in the Vitthala temple at Vijayanagara praise the king for the gift of pot of gold, *ānandanidhi* in August c.1539 C.E. It is likely that the most likely gift-giving event would be that of *ānandanidhi* performed in c. 1539 C.E. as Achyutaraya is said to have performed it several times. The gift of *ānandanidhi*, meaning a pot of gold made to the learned *brāhmanas* involved pots made of *udambara* wood filled with precious stones and coins of gold, silver or copper. It was performed in c. 1533 C.E. and in c. 1539 C.E. when gifts were given to *brāhmanas*. But the *ānandanidhi* gift of c. 1539 C.E has been mentioned in seven of his nine gift-giving inscriptions at Vijayanagara. They have been mentioned twice in the Krishnaswamy temple, twice in the Achyutaraya temple (one of these is on the *gôpura* of the temple), once in the Pattabhirama temple, once in the Cikkahude temple and once in the Vitthala temple. By this gift of c. 1539 C.E. Achyutaraya is said to have made the *brāhmanas* equal to Kubera, the god of wealth and the merit accruing from this ceremony is said to be longevity, perfect health and imperial sovereignty.[30] Furthermore, the gift of c. 1539 C.E. was to secure the imperial sovereignty not for the king, but for his son. As the temple was built and consecrated in c. 1539 C.E. when the particular gift was made, the gift-giving scene on the pillar must have been carved at that time. The fact that the figures are not as well-finished as the other figures in the shrine supports the view that they must have been carved within a short time.

Thus, it is most likely that the gift-giving scene depicts the *ānandanidhi* gift of c. 1539 C.E. The reason for making large gifts soon after his accession to the throne might be sought in the list of contenders for the throne. Perhaps, he wished to secure his throne by securing the good will of his nobles and chiefs and to strengthen his claim over it as he was not the son and immediate heir of Krishnadevaraya. In fact, the throne had been threatened by Ramaraya, the son-in-law of Krishnadevaraya. After the demise of Krishnadevaraya, there was a controversy about accession and Achyutaraya is said to have been crowned thrice,[31] first at Tirupati as soon as he heard the news of his brother's death, second at Kalahasti and the third time at the capital.[32] As the position of the king was uncertain (especially with Rama Raja as the contender to the throne), it was perhaps appropriate to make a large number of gifts to gain additional popularity and status in order to secure his throne.[33] Whether the scene depicts a specific event or not, what is obvious is that the portrait was sculpted for the specific purpose of showing his liberal nature and enhancing his prestige in the capital and visual imagery substantiated the ideological powers of gift giving.

There is a unique stone structure in the city of Vijayanagara, the Balance, locally known as the Tulabhara, located near the Vitthala temple (Pl.5.). The structure consists of two pillars that support a central beam. It has provisions to hang a balance which was probably made of metal and was used in the ritual of gift-giving, and was especially used to make large gifts or *mahādānas*. Constructed for the purpose of weighing the king in gold or precious stones, an equal amount of gold was distributed to the people and *brāhmanas* through temples. It was constructed by Krishnadevaraya after his victory over the Gajapatis of Orissa for the purpose of weighing the king against gold and precious stones to be gifted to *brāhmanas* and continued to be used by subsequent kings. On the base of the structure is a group of figures and based on iconographical evidences and the architectural context, it is that of Krishnadeva Raya and his two queens Chnna Devi and Tirumala Devi. The identification is also based upon the degree of iconographical resemblance to the royal (inscribed) portrait images of Krishnadeva Raya and his two wives in the Pratima Mandapa in the northern entrance of the gateway of the Tirumalai Temple at Tirupati.[34]

Among the numerous *mahādānas* such as *tulādāna*, *mahāpurushdāna, suvarnamerudāana, asvadāna, gajadāna, bhudāna , kannikadāna* mentioned in the inscriptions, two most frequent ones cited in the inscriptions are the *tulāpurushdāna*, when the king was weighed against gold and *hiranyagarbhadāna* the gifting of gold in the form of a golden embryo. The *tulāpurushadāna* was performed by Krishnadeva Raya, Achyuta Raya and Deva Raya.[35] Vira Narasingaraya is said to have performed *dānas*, such as the *tuladāna, mahāpurushdāna, suvaranamerudāna, asvadāana, gajadāna, godāna, bhudāna , kannikadāna and brahmapratisthadāna.*[36] In fact, before abducting the throne, he is said to have performed ten *dānas*, sixteen *mahādānas*, as well as the *suvarnatula*, weighing oneself against gold, and *mauktikatula,* weighing oneself against pearls. Even as late as during the time of Venkata III, learned *brāhmanas* were anointed or abundantly provided with gold by Venkata.[37]

The large gifts to *brāhmanas* had also political and social motives. It was a means to sustain the class, accept their superior status, and once again maintain the caste system. Gifting sustained the caste which supported kingly values and meant the recognition of the *brāhmana* who was the womb of kingly power.[38] In exchange, the *brāhmana* who came near the cultural concept of god, upheld royalty, accorded political legitimization especially at the time of coronations, bestowed honors, titles, and support to the king. Apart from the role of royal gifting being a mode of achieving legitimacy, it placed the *brāhmana* in a network of relationships and social control with the temple and king, all of whom had a community of interest which was conducive to the temple and brought them close in an active transactional relationship. The system of bestowing prestige and titles upon the givers was practiced on smaller *rājas* or *nāyakas* as well, who imitated the kings activity and received titles and honor through the temples. An instance may be seen in the imagery of Rayana Raja (Pl.7) on the gateway of the Virupaksha temple.

Considering the tendency of local leaders to identify with the royal capital, the images of local *nāyakas* (who rendered military support) in Vijayanagara temples, attest the fact that they gained a portrait or temple honor as exchange for temple gifting. In fact, loyalty to Vijayanagara rulers depended on displays of piety through religious gifting and prestige was reciprocally bestowed on the givers. Like the Vijayanagara royal family, high ranking courtiers, as well, made spectacular donations. The importance of donors for the maintenance and existence of temples was duly recognized and a large number of portraits of patrons were depicted in the vicinity of temples. Portraits of some of these secondary royal donors are found in the courtyard of the Virupaksha temple (Pl.8). Although it is not possible to identify these donors as those of specific individuals they could represent those in the palace, nobles and their wives, local chieftains, or other royal functionaries. Their depiction was, in fact, a recognition of their importance for the maintenance of the temples similar to the according of food and garland honors.[39] That they were depicted on visually powerful spaces of architecture leads us to conclude that they played a key socio-economic role in the network system.

Symbolic Value of Gifting

The Vijayanagara king was also dependent on the construction of relationships with local power holders and *nayakas*. Religious gifting to temples specifically provided foci for collective worship thereby creating important regional arenas for political interaction among extra-local sovereigns, leaders of local religious sectarian leaders. There was a vertical and horizontal integration of kings, local leaders, *brāhmanas* and the main actor in this new expansion was the *brāhmana* connected with the temple. However, the main initiators were the kings and the (imitative) secular donors who added to the growing system of social alliances.

The Vijayanagara kings were identified with the images of a protector, provider and largess. As mentioned above, they announced their performance of gift ceremonies proclaiming their beneficence. This concept of the king as the most generous, who tried to bestow the good things in life to the people, is very clearly revealed in the contemporary historical text, *Madhura Vijaya* in which king Bukkaraya advises the prince to keep the people happy and to give gifts, as the people were the wealth of the nation.[40] On a public level, the king was an administrative hero and an embodiment of social generosity. Gifting was a means of obtaining status but more importantly, it promoted social solidarity. He was also the royal protector of righteousness in the material world and as a protector, he was divine in the eyes of the people. The Vijayanagara kings were the greatest devotee confirmed by royal portraits of Krishnadevaraya in the northern entrance gate of the Tirupati temple, the portraits of Krishnadevaraya in the Krishnaswamy temple (Pl.6) similar to that of Rajaraja as Somaskanda (the chief worshipper) in the Chola temple.

Royal patronage of temples were gift giving acts, and were *dharmic* acts of kingship similar to the building of tanks and other civic structures by the king for the public good. The Balance was used to weigh the king against gold or precious stones which were gifted to the people, *brāhmanas* and others. This structure, located near the Vitthala temple and on the important road between the palace area and the temple cities or *puras* acted as a visual reminder of the generosity and largess of the kings. It substantiated the fact that kings institutionalized the great ritual gift-giving as a ceremonial event and was both a royal and a religious act. Royal cum religious ceremonies, such as the Mahanavami played an important role is attested by the secular structure, Mahanavami Dibba at Vijayanagara. Such an analysis of the close linkage between the royal, sacred and material or rather king, temple and guild (market)—in terms of built environment, ideology, performance, function and ritual celebration—is antithetical to the recent interpretations of the royal and sacred from the archaeological evidences at Vijayanagara (Hampi).

Although the balance portraits are small, the symmetrical structure of the Balance was a powerful symbol of the generosity of the king. For the first time in South Indian history, a permanent stone structure for royal gifting was built which meant the institutionalization of the practice of royal liberality. Necessitated by the changing political ideology, religion and societal changes, especially the Islamic kingdoms and the *nayaka* power, there was a transformation in the character and pattern of royal gifting which was substantiated by gift giving imagery. The king visually reaffirmed his superiority and autonomy as the pre-eminent person in the kingdom, subject to no one, ruler of all, as one who enjoyed the exclusive right to give gifts. The Balance was both sculpture and architecture, thorough which the king had the power to impress and advertise his liberality and ceremonial role. However, the reason for this architectural Balance to be large and the scale of the gifting imagery of Achyutaraya to be small is perhaps due to many reasons: one being, the latter was in a temple context and the king could not be accorded more importance in the context of the temple, meaning god. Hence they were placed on pillars, and gateways; while in a secular context, it played a role similar to the large free standing portraits of kings and queens found at Vijayanagara near the palaces (Pls.9, 10).[41] The relief portrait of Achyutaraya appears to be a religious statement made in the context of the temple-god relationship. That is, the king's relief portraits presents the role of the king within the temple, a role that is necessary to the temple's completeness and function and do not have to be large, they are not political or propagandistic statements. Similarly, the Balance portraits are not important in themselves to the viewer; it is the message of imperial liberality of kingship that is intended. The relief one is an iconographical representation of the view of religious authority towards kingship, the Balance one is the king's conception about his concept of *dāna*, *dharma*, and protection.

Royal gifting was an act of devotion and *dharma*, but was colored with an awareness of its material and symbolic value. It sustained the temple which was a citadel of economic power and an instrument of authority. Gifting was initiated by imperial power; it stimulated a complex system of network alliances which in turn sustained a redistributive economy. Ostentatious gifts increased political stability and social order that affirmed the ethics of obligation and reciprocity and enhanced the sanctity of Vijayanagara kingship.

Notes and References

1 James Heitzman, *Gifts of Power: Lordship in an Early Indian state* (Oxford: Oxford University Press, New Delhi, 1997), 145 ff.

2 Ronald Inden, Ritual Authority and cyclical Time in Hindu Kingship, in *Kingship and Authority in South Asia*, ed., J. F. Richards (Madison: University of Wisconsin, 1978), 28-73.

3 Dirks, *The Hollow Crown: Ethnohistory of an Indian Kingdom* (Cambridge: Cambridge University Press, 1987), 37.

4 Ibid., *The Hollow crow,:* 28, 370.

5 Arjun Appadurai: *Worship and Conflict under Colonial Rule: A South Indian Case* (Cambridge: Cambridge University Press, 1981), 84 ff.

6 J. D. M. Derret, *Religion Law and the State in India* (London: Faber and Faber, 1968), 486.

7 *SII* 4, no. 259.; *EI* 1, 361-371.

8 In an inscription of 1405, the opening genealogy includes the statement that his (Bukkaraja's) son is King Harihara, who equals *sutraman* (Indra) in power and who, being devoted to the performance of the sixteen great gifts, has destroyed the sins of the Kali age. *EI* 3, 224- 230.

9 James Heitzman, op.cit., 145.

10 Villages of Devasamudra were no longer paying taxes to the temple as prescribed in the inscription of c.1557 C.E.

11 A fixed share of produce or fixed rent on land.

12 The temple honored such individuals who made large gifts or appointed them to key posts.

13 Heinzman, op. cit., 108.

14 *S.I.I.* No 227; *A.R.* no 48 of 1889.

15 The temple invested the surplus back into its own local region.

16 John Dowson, *The History of India as told by its own Historians. The Muhammedan Period. Edited from the posthumous papers of the late SirElliot by John Dowson.* 8 Vols. (London: Trubner,1867) Reprint (Allahbad: Kitab Mahal, 1969).(For Account of Abd-er-Razaaq, Vol. 4 (1872),107; Robert Sewell, *A Forgotten Empire Vijayanaga): A Contribution to the History of India* (London: Swan Sonnenschein & Co., 1900). Reprint (New Delhi:Asian Educational Services, 1983), 255.

17 Duarte Barbosa, *An Account of the Countries Bordering on the Indian Ocean and* their Inhabitants written by Duarte Barbosa and completed about the year 1518 *A.D.*Translated, edited and annotated by M. Longsworth Dames, 2 Vols. Works of the Hakluyt Society (London: 1918-21. Reprint, New Delhi: 1967), 200-202.

18 Elliot, op. cit., 23

19 Channabasapp S. Patil, Pre-Vijahyanagar Temples at Hampi, in *Vijayanagara: Progress of Research* 1987-88, eds.,Devaraj, D.V and Patil, (Directorate of Archaeology and Museums, Mysore, 1991),113-142.

20 Vasundhara Filliozat, The Town-Planning of Vijayangara, *AARP* 14 (Dec. 1978), 54-64.

21 Sewell, op.cit., 246, 247. Those who traded in articles of sandalwood or sandal paste called *gamdhada*. *SII*, VolIX, pt. ii. No. 566; *ARIE* no. 10, of 1904.

22 *EC* IV,YI,61 *EC*, V *AK*. 68; Vii, *SK* 313; B.Muddachari, *Economic History of Karnataka*(Mysore: Udaya Prakashan,1982), 22.

23 *Santhes* were organized fairs which took place in twenty six towns of the Vijayanagra empire.

24 *Banjiga* stands for the original words, *banija*, vanijya meaning merchant or trader. An inscription of Harihara II mentions that various sects depend on them and they were present during the time of tax agreement with the Vijayanagara government. *E.C.* V. Bl 75. After the agreement was reached it was circulated among all members of different trading centers and they were informed of the taxes. In the city of Vijayanagara, the chief of customs, *muddeya dannāyaka*, discussed the rates of taxes to be collected from and paid by the Salu Mule Banajigas to Vijayanagara treasury. The importance of the guild can be seen in the title, of *prithwisettitana* or mayoralty of the earth conferred on the president. Muddachari,op.cit., 24. It appears that the king acted as a protector to traders and collected revenues indirectly through the revenue collecting assemblies.

25 The Salu Mule Banajigas had their organizations in many other towns.

26 Burton Stein, Reapproaching Vijayanagara, in *Studies of South India: An Anthology of Recent Research and Scholarship*, ed., Robert E. Frykenberg and Pauline Kolenda (Madras and New Delhi: New Era Publications and American Institute of Indian Studies, 1985) , 31-50.

27 Nalini Rao, Royal Portraits at Vijayanagara: Identification and Meaning, in *New Trends in Indian Art and Archaeology,* Vol 2.,eds., B. U. Nayak and N.C. Ghosh (Aditya Prakashan. New Delhi, 1992), 349-368.

28 Acyutaraya is said to have had Raghunatha, the poet, bathed in gold and precious stones, *kanakaratnabhisekham*, unction with gold and pearls, after he wrote the poem *Parijatapaharana* in six hours as mentioned in the *Sahityaratnakara* by Yoganarayana Dikshita. Aiyangar, *Sources of Vijayanagara History*, 270.

29 *SII* 9, pt. 2, nos. 557 and 558.

30 The purpose of the gift is enumerated by Hemadri in the Dasakhanda of his *Chaturvarga Chintamani*. Ruth Sheilavardhini Sathyanathan, Achyuta

Raya. Unpublished Ph. D. dissertation. (Karnatak University, Dharwar, 1977), 61-62.

31 Confirmed by the *Achyutarayabhyudayam*. Sathyanathan, op.cit., 3. In the inscription of Ankavalli Sorab Taluk, dated c.1529 C.E., the donor made a grant in order that Acyutaraya might be established in the empire. See N.Venkataramanayya, *Studies in the Third Dynasty of Vijayanagara* (Madras: Madras University of Madras, 1936), 14.

32 Krishnaswami Aiyangar, *Sources of Vijayanagar History*, ed.(Madras: University of Madras, 1919. Reprint, Delhi: Gian Publishing House, 1986), 161.

33 In the inscription of Ankavalli Sorab Taluk, dated 1529, the donor made a grant in order that Acyutaraya might be established in the empire. N. Venkataramanayya, *Studies in the Third Dynasty of Vijayanagara* (Madras: Madras University of Madras, 1936), 14.

34 Sri Sadhu Subrahmanya Sastry, *Tirupati Sri Venkatesvara Tirupati* (Tirumalai Tirupati) Devasthanams, 1981: 211.

35 *EC*, 1919, nos. 511, 543, 546.

36 Mentioned in the *Kongudesarajakkalin Caritram*, 16-6-9.

37 *EI* 3, 236, 258.

38 Louis Dumont: The Conception of Kingship in Ancient India, in *Religion, Politics and History in India*. Collected Papers in Indian Sociology (Paris: Mouton Publishers, 1970), 62-88.

39 Heitzman, *op.cit.*,181.

40 Shanbhag, *Gangadeviya Madhura Vijaya* (Dharwar: Karnataka Viswavidyalaya, 1964), 5 ff.

41 Nalini Rao, *Royal Artistic Imagery at Vijayanagara* (New Delhi: Munshiram Manoharlal) (Forthcoming).

Description of Plates

1. View of Vijayanagara showing the bazaar street
2. Shrine in Tiruvengalanatha temple complex, Vijayanagara
3. Achyutaraya on a pillar, Tiruvengalanatha temple

4a. Achyutaraya giving a gift, Vijayanagara

4b. Details of 4a

5. The King's Balance, Vijayanagara
6. Portraits of Krishnadevaraya, Krishnaswamy temple
7. Rayana Raja, Virupaksha temple
8. Donors, Virupaksha temple
9. Torso of a king, Vijayanagara Museum
10. Excavated remains, Rangashala, Royal center, Vijayanagara

Nailini Rao: 1. View of Vijayanagara showing the bazaar street

Nailini Rao: 2. Shrine in Tiruvengalanatha temple complex, Vijayanagara

Nailini Rao: 3. Achyutaraya on a pillar, Tiruvengalanatha temple

Nailini Rao: 4a. Achyutaraya giving a gift, Vijayanagara

Nailini Rao: 4b. Details of 4a

Nailini Rao: 5. The King's Balance, Vijayanagara

Nailini Rao: 6. Portraits of Krishnadevaraya, Krishnaswamy temple

Nailini Rao: 7. Rayana Raja, Virupaksha temple

Nailini Rao: 8. Donors, Virupaksha temple

Nailini Rao: 9. Torso of a king, Vijayanagara Museum

Nailini Rao: 10. Excavated remains, Rangashala, Royal center, Vijayanagara

7

Being in Love with God is not Enough: Social Reform by Basavanna Through *Bhakti*

Deepak Shimkhada

The discourse on Shiva *bhakti* in Vijayanagara must begin with Basavanna,[1] the founder of Veerashaivism and the author of many *Vachanas* (poems or sayings). His vision appears to have played a fundamental role in shaping the character of Veerashaivism,[2] which is the main focus of this paper. Here I will examine the early years of Basavanna, his upbringing, the milieu in which he grew up, his belief in *Kudala Sangama Deva* (Lord of the Meeting Rivers), and finally his theology based on this god whom he considered his *ishtadévata or* personal deity. The Lord of the Meeting Rivers was none other than Shiva, who, of course, came to serve as the underlying epitomy of Veerashaivism. It is my hope that at the end of the paper a full portrait of Veerashaivism, founded by Basavanna, will become clear, allowing the viewer to see the true character of the religion in which falling in love with God was not enough. A follower of Veerashaivism could or was expected to do More. What is this, More, I will examine with the help of the theology of Basavanna as reflected through his *Vachanas*.

The Beginnings: Textual Context

The love for Shiva can be traced to the mythological tales of Sati wanting to marry him. The love that was inseparable between Shiva and Sati is amply illustrated by the story in which Sati desires Shiva so much so that she goes out of her way to please him by performing physical austerities in the forms of meditation, fasting, penance, and ritual worship. These severe austerities described in the *Puranas*[3] are no doubt a form of self sacrifice to which I will return later while discussing Sati and the unorthodox behavior of Basavanna. The Puranic tale shows that hard work performed with single-mindedness can pay off, because after performing austerities for many years, Sati does win the love of Shiva.

After marriage, like all newly-wed couples, Shiva and Sati retired to a honeymoon suite. However, they failed to emerge out of the suite for thousands of years, causing imbalance in the cosmic cycles. Hence, they had to be persuaded to come out of their suite.[4] The erotic dalliance between Shiva and Sati can be seen as a love that binds the couple into eternal unity. As all good things must come to an end, so did their union, but not their love. One day, Sati found out that her father Dakshya was performing a grand *ashwamédha Yajna* or horse sacrifice to which both Shiva and Sati were not invited. Out of curiosity, Sati decided to go to her father to find out the reason, against the wishes of Shiva. But at the *yajna* Sati's father Dakshya insulted Shiva; Sati, unable to bear the pain of her husband being insulted publicly in front of 330 million gods jumped into the *agnikunda* or the ritual fire pit, which her father had built. Thus, Sati killed herself out of intense love for her husband. According to the story narrated in most Puranic sources,[5] Shiva wandered the earth carrying the lifeless body of Sati. Because the distraught Siva would not part with the lifeless body of Sati, it was cut up by Vishnu into fifty-one pieces,[6] causing the body to fall so that Siva would stop wandering.

This story shows the unconditional love between the divine couple, a love far beyond ordinary measure. The love made them bind as one, for one could not live without the other. Sati killing herself unable to hear the slander lodged against her husband was the basis of the myth in which Shiva showed his devotion to his beloved. So distraught was he at the loss of his wife that he did not remain himself. Blinded by his love for Sati, Shiva was unable to think or act, wandering around aimlessly carrying the lifeless body of Sati. Even in separation, they were one; Shiva united physically with the lifeless body of Sati, while in reality, Shiva was just *shava*, a walking dead man.

When one speaks of Bhakti movement in Hinduism, one usually thinks of Vaishnavism, because it is widely known and well documented. The Shiva *bhakti* movement is, however, less known and differs radically from Vaishnavism. It is this difference that makes Veerashaivism stand out as unique. Where do we begin looking for this uniqueness?

The Origins of Veerashaivism

One place to look for the origin of Veerashaivism, especially in the cult of the *linga*, is in the ancient Indus Valley. From here have come a *linga* and small seals bearing images of man with representation of an erect phallus. A follower of Veerashaivism is also called *Lingayat*, the bearer of *linga*, because the person wears a small *linga* around his/her neck or chest. The intent is to keep the *linga*, his *ishtadévata,* with him/her at all times. Hence, wearing a *linga* on the body is a mark of commitment or devotion. Although no further anthropological evidences other than those mentioned earlier have been found, it is likely that the origins of the Lingayat may be traced to the ancient past. Thousands of years later, Lingayat, as a religion, reached its height under the leadership of Basavanna in Bagevadi, his hometown in Vijayanagara.

A. K. Ramanujan in his seminal work on Veerashaivism in South India compares two words – *sthavara* and *jangama*[7] – terms central to understanding Veerashaivism, using the *Vachana* of Basavanna:

The rich
will make temple for Shiva.
what shall I,
a poor man,
do?

My legs are pillars,
the body the shrine,
the head a cupola
of gold.

Listen, O lord of the meeting rivers,
things standing shall fall,
but the moving ever shall stay.

-Basavanna: 820

It is evident that Basavanna in this *Vachana* compares a temple to his body in a similar manner that a Hindu temple is traditionally built in the image of the body of a *mahāpurusha*. The next concept that the poet introduces is equally significant; he speaks of the transitory nature of a monument and the ever-lasting nature of that which moves.

We may ask, what is this Ever-Lasting nature of a temple to which Basavanna refers. Let us examine the structure of a temple to illustrate his metaphor. A temple has wings and arms which are called the *hasta* or hands and pillars, *pada* or feet. The top of the temple is *shikhara* or head.[8] The innermost sanctum, the darkest part of the temple, is the *garbhagriha* or womb chamber, in which is placed the icon of the deity. Because Basavanna was a Shaivite, a Lingayat in particular, his temple must carry a *linga* in the *garbhagriha*. If we take the temple as *sthavara*, that does not move, then the *linga* is *jangama* that moves. That which does not move can fall and get destroyed, and what moves remains permanent. This sounds like a riddle that needs further explanation to understand its intended meaning. From reading his biography we know that Basavanna was sympathetic to the cause of the poor and downtrodden. Though he was of Brahman caste himself, he fought to bring equality to the people of the Shudra caste, making him a great social reformer.

The metaphor of a temple could stand for the rich. Ramanujan states that Medieval South Indian temples looked remarkably like palaces with battlements that were richly endowed and patronized by the wealthy and the powerful, without whom the massive structures housing the bejeweled gods and sculptured pillars would not have been possible.[9] Such temples with battlement-like structures were symbols of wealth and power which in their heydays stood like monoliths unmovable, protected by the rulers. But when the power of the patrons waned, the temples became the targets of invaders, who often sacked and pillaged, even destroyed them so that they crumbled leaving only the remnants or the vestiges of their glorious past. No matter under what glorious circumstances the temples were built, they could not live forever, for they were subject to dissolution either by the ravages of time or invaders. However, an idea, a concept, tradition in the form of *dharma* or charity lived long like a moving *jangama*, it was immortal.[10]

A temple, thus, can be taken as a metaphor of the rich, because it stays in one place, *achal* or fixed like a pillar, unwilling to move or bend to the changes of time. In contrast, the poor person has no fixed place to live, always keeps moving from one place tot the next looking for work or food, willing to do anything that will put food on the table. Although the poor kept moving, the virtue of the poor, as quality, stayed fixed. On the other hand the rich though they had wealth, large houses came crashing down when the economic and political tides changed against their favor.

In the view of Basavanna, the *sthavara* and *jangama* are to be understood in these metaphorical contexts. Ramanujan, hence, emphatically states that what is made (in the case of a temple) will crumble, what is standing will fall; but what is living moving *jangama*, is immortal.[11] Similarly, *shivalinga* enshrined in the sanctum of a temple is eternal like the *jangama* when understood from the perspective just described. A *linga* is a concept of Shiva principle, a dynamic one in that, and as a dynamic principle, it is fluid; and yet, it is eternal.

Going Against the Established Traditions

Basavanna lived in a time of Brahmanic hegemony. From reading his *Vachanas*, he appears to be a man who was troubled by his own high caste status. Though born as a Brahman, he was not proud of calling himself a Brahman, because he had seen an unflattering side of the Brahman caste. He was not hesitant to speak against the Brahman, as the three *Vachanas* below will demonstrate:

How is it, Lord, that the Brahmans do not practice what they preach? (574)

Loaded with the burden of the Vedas, the Brahman is a veritable donkey. (586)

Those of the Brahman caste are teachers, is a lie. (599)

Basavanna was a true visionary, in spite of being a Brahman and in spite of living in the twelfth century. He pushed for equality of all people, regardless of their caste. He urged everyone to believe in Shiva, because he is the god of countless lower caste people who serve the upper three castes. According to the Lingayats, *linga* represents Brahman, the highest principle of the universe and as Brahman, the *linga* is part of every living being. *Candrājnagama Kriyāpada*, a Shaivite text, states that from which the universe is evolved and that in which it is dissolved is the *linga* the eternal Brahman. This text goes one step further, asserting that the creation and dissolution of the universe takes place in the Brahman which is called *Linga*.[12]

The *ishtadévata*, the *Kudala Sangama Deva* (Lord of the Meeting Rivers) was personified Shiva, whom Basavanna visualized as more brilliant than a thousand suns, incomprehensible yet blissful which renders him speechless.[13] It is evident from the writings of Basavanna that all of his *Vachanas* were dedicated to Shiva, whom he called the Lord of the Meeting Rivers, which, too, is moving by the virtue of flowing, and yet is ever-lasting, like the *jangama*, the poor, the downtrodden. Thus, the cult of the *linga* which Basavanna advocated was at the heart of Lingayats of Veerashaivism.

Bhakti, The Soteriological Surrender

Bhakti has been considered as one of the *margas* or paths to reach god, practiced by many in India. But whereas the Vaishnava *bhakti* movement was distinctive of the Northern Indian landscape, the Siva *bhakti* movement was primarily native of South India.[14] *Bhakti* movements which swept most of Indian subcontinent especially during the medieval period have received a great deal of attention from scholars. The reason for this is that *bhakti* has influenced virtually all aspects of Indian religion,[15] and, in fact, all aspects of Indian life. However, in contrast to Vaishnava *bhakti* movement, Shiva *bhakti* movement has received less attention, not because it was an unimportant movement, but because its followers were fewer in number and were confined primarily to regions of South India. Nevertheless, the Shiva *bhakti* movement was no less significant in terms of the impact it made on its followers, their art, culture, and literature. This becomes evident when we examine some of the *Vachanas* composed by Basavanna.

Before we go into the history of *bhakti* movements in India, it is necessary to understand what inspired the movement in the first place. Understood generally as a quick path to God, the *bhakti* path emphasized devotion. The Vedic rituals on the other hand were shunned by the followers of the *bhakti* movements because they were presided over by priests who acted as intermediaries between the devotees and the gods. The *bhaktimarga* was open to all who wanted to walk on it. All they had to do was to embrace god with love and devotion, claiming him as master. Although it is a master-slave relationship, the god could also be approached in the form of a lover as in the case of Mira Bai and some others. Because the *bhakti* movement was originally conceived as a reaction against Vedic rituals and Brahmanic hegemony, the followers were primarily of the Shudra caste who were denied equality in Hindu society. Economic and religious disparities in society directly affected people of the Shudra caste. The *bhakti* movement provided a shift that gave the lower caste Hindus opportunity to rise up and elevate themselves from the bottom. The hope was that they, too, could gain soteriological freedom from the caste bondage in which they were eternally fettered. The *bhaktimarga* offered the exit they were seeking. K. Ishwaran makes a convincing case when he states the following in support of the new shift that emerged as a result of the Vaishnava *bhakti* movement in North India:

> The desired shift from dirty occupations to clean occupations, from polluted caste to purer caste, from a life of filth to a life of cleanliness, from bondage to *karma* to liberation from *karma*, dominated the aspirations of the people. They found that the *bhakti* way was the only way they could hope to realize such aspirations. For them, it was an easy mode, and the only mode, of emotional realization in life, requiring no complex intellectual solution. All that it seemed to require was a passionate devotion to the deity in the temple, a concentrated meditation on, and love for it articulated in a frenzy of emotion, which took the form of dancing or singing.[16]

From the above description and from what one can witness when one visits a Krishna temple in America, the intensity of *bhakti* and passionate devotion of devotees becomes evident as the sound, smell, and sight fill the temple. These crystallize in various forms of art, music, poetry, drama, costume, and in the preparation of food and the performance of *puja*. However, for *Shiva* the outpourings of *bhakti* could be expressed through pure love, without rites and rituals. This is where the Vaishnavites and Shaivites differ in their respective *bhaktimarga*.

Basavanna, as we gleaned from accounts of his early years in Bagevadi, grew up among the Shudras, who were denied the privilege of seeking Siva in the company of higher castes.[17] As a person of social conscience, Basavanna must have found flaws in the system and he appears to have revolted against it. A distinction is made between the *desi* and *mārga* traditions.[18] As the two words connote, *desi* refers to little tradition that is local, and *mārga* refers to great tradition that is based on Vedic principles followed by the majority of the people of the upper castes. Basavanna, now at the forefront of the *desi* tradition, represented the poor and downtrodden, and clashed with those of the *marga* tradition with his *Vachanas* as weapons. He expresses his *bhakti* to Shiva, the Lord of the Meeting Rivers, through his poems in the form of *Vachana*, in which he prays to Shiva, questions him, negotiates with him, glorifies him, and even accuses him. But most of all, Basavanna does not go to Shiva temple, nor does he offer *puja*, or perform sacrifice. And yet,

Basavanna in his own way was the biggest *bhakta* of all times, earning the title of *bhaktibhandāri* (treasure house of devotion) from some Basava scholars.[19] However, Ishwaran argues that the devotion of Basavanna cannot be taken as *bhakti*, but rather *sharana*.[20]

It is true that Basavanna did not believe either in Vedic rituals or the Vaishnavite method of *bhakti*. But it is equally true that he loved his god and had deep devotion for him like the Vaishnava or Shaivite followers. At the core, he was a true *bhakta*, a devotee, who, like Sati as in the Puranic story narrated in the beginning of this essay, was willing to give up anything to please his god Shiva. From the movement he initiated to bring the poor and downtrodden within the belief system of Veerashaivism, it appears that Basavanna was more interested in the soteriological deliverance of others than of himself. Can he be called a savior? Is there a twist in his brand of *bhakti*? It certainly appears so if we examine carefully his unorthodox actions. First, Basavanna must have realized the boundless love and grace of Shiva, as becomes evident from the mythological story cited earlier in which Shiva quickly becomes pleased with the prayers of his devotee, and also quickly loves his devotee, Sati. Losing her he quickly abandons everything and mourns her loss. Here is a god who loves, as much as if not more than his own devotee.

> If I say, I love You, I trust You, surrender to You
> You will test me by shaking my body.
> You will test me by shaking my mind.
> You will test me by shaking my riches.
> Kudalasangamadeva, You tremble at devotion
> Fearless of such tests!
>
> -Basavanna: 214

Basavanna must have realized that doing Good to others leads one closer to god, and hence the notion of *dasoha* (doing good to the community) is so paramount in his movement. The act of *dasoha* takes place when one gives to charity or performs certain philanthropic acts more for the benefit of the community than for oneself. While performing *dasoha* one receives rewards many times greater than doing for oneself. That was the philosophy which Basavanna must have believed, and thus his brand of *bhakti* was different. It stood out as so unique it was called *sharana* by some. No matter by what name it is called, it is *bhakti* directed toward his personal god Kudalasangamadeva, Shiva, who was without form and quality. Hence, the humanism that Basavanna expressed through his brand of *bhakti* was without form and quality. It was an expression of pure love performed with the intent of pleasing his *ishtadevata*.

I am here reminded of a film titled, Pay it Forward which I watched some years ago. In it a boy in school receives a social studies assignment. The purpose of the assignment was to find an idea that will improve mankind. The boy decides to do three good deeds for someone and they in turn can "pay it forward" and so forth, resulting into positive changes in the community. If the trend is caught up by others, it could prove infectious and change the entire society. Was Basavanna trying to do the same for the community in which he lived by improving the quality of the poor and downtrodden people of the Shudra caste with the Shiva *bhakti* he had embraced?

Some nine hundred years after the death of Basavanna, the Veerashaivism he started as a *bhakti* movement in Vijayanagara appears to have continued without interruption, just as a river flows and merges into the ocean.[21] Finally, the dynamic principle of *jangama* Basavanna advocated comes to fruition in the form of *bhakti* for *Kudalasangamadeva*, his *ishtadevata*, who is Shiva in the form of *linga*.

Notes and References

1 Also called Basava for short. See K. Ishwaran, *Speaking of Basava, Lingayat Religion and Culture in South Asia*. (Boulder: Westview Press, 1992).

2 Ramanujan, A.K., *Speaking of Siva*. New York: Penguin Books, 1979 (Reprinted); Also see Dan A. Chekki, *Religion and Social System of the Virasaiva Community* (Connecticut: Greenwood Press, 1997).

3 See *Devi Gita*, Translated by Swami Satyananda Saraswati(Delhi: Motilal Banarsidas, 1991); *Skanda Purana*, translated by G.V. Tagare. (Motilal Banarsidass Publishers, 1993); *Siva Purana*, translated by J.L.Shastri. Motilal (Banarsidass, 1986).

4 According to the story, the fire god Agni was sent at the request of other gods to break up their love making. For interrupting their love making, the angry Siva curses Agni with a curse.

5 *The Srimad Devi Bhagavatam*, Translated by Swami Vijnanananda. New Delhi: Munshiram Manoharlal, 1977. *Devi Gita*, Translated by Swami Satyananda Saraswati (Delhi: Motilal Banarsidas, 1991). See also *The Devi Gita, The Song of the Goddess: A Translation, Annotation, and Commentary* translated by C. Mackenzie Brown (Albany: State University of New York Press, 1998). In this version Guhyeswari is referred to as Guhyekali. See p. 241, 8:11.

6 The number of body parts of Sati varies from 51 to 108 based on which Puranic source one uses. However, number 51 appears to be more common than 108 and, hence I prefer to use that number here.

7 Ramanujan, Op. Cit., p. 20.

8 Ibid.

9 Ibid., p. 21.

10 Ibid.

11 Ibid.

12 Cited by G.V. Tagare in *Slavism: Some Glimpses*. New Delhi: D.K. Printworld, 1996, p. 111.

13 Ibid., p. 106.

14 Bailey, G.M., *Bhakti Studies*. New Delhi: Sterling Publishers Private Limited, 1992; Also see *Medieval Bhakti Movements in India* by Narendra Nath Bhattacharyya.(New Delhi: Munshiram Manoharlal Publishers, 1989).

15 Ibid., p. 1.

16 Ishwaran, K., *Speaking of Basava, Lingayat Religion and Culture in South Asia* (Boulder: Westview Press, 1992), p. 7.

17 Ibid.

18 Ibid., p. 2

19 Ibid., p. 114

20 Ibid., p. 111

21 According to Deccan Herald report, more than 1,000 members of the Jatav community, a Dalit sub-caste, took *ishtalinga deekshe* in the capital on October, 20, 2003, for equal religious rights. At the ceremony held under Veerasaiva organizations and Delhi Pradesh Jatav Mahasabha, the Jatavs were accorded *lingadharane* and were given *Basava siddhantha pratijna vidhi and Basava dharma suthra* by several religious leaders from the Lingayat community headed by Dr. Thontada Siddalinga swamiji of Dambola math. Dr. Siddalinga swamiji said by according *lingadharane*, the maths were fulfilling the objectives of social reformer Basavanna of bringing equality in society. Out of about two million Jatavs in Delhi alone, those who took *deekshe* today included men, women and children from the Jatav community. The devotees were administered the Sri Guru Basavasiddhantha bodhe by Mahantha Swamiji of Chittaragi math.

8

Contribution of the Vijayanagara Kings to the Study of the *Vedas*

S.R. Rao

One of the great contributions of the Vijayanagara empire to the promotion of Sanskrit culture is the translation of the *Vedas* and the elaborate commentaries and interpretations by Sayana. The *Vedas* which contained the germ ideas of Hindu theology, philosophy, ritual and doctrines were subject to varied interpretations. During the medieval period, due to political and social upheavals, the *Vedas* were in need of a meaningful interpretation and commentary. This was undertaken by *āchāryas* and learned Sanskrit scholars in South Indian religious institutions. Royal patronage to educational institutions became an important concern of the Vijayanagara rulers especially in the background of Islamic invasions and destruction of Hindu temples.

The first part of the paper deals with the historicity of the *Vedic* language; the ideas and concepts which has often been misunderstood as unhistorical or imaginative. By corroborating Vedic linguistic evidences with archaeological evidences obtained in the Indus Valley sites, it is possible to understand the dynamism and richness of Sanskrit which had helped the development of vernacular languages, especially Kannada and Telugu during the period under review. This essay is a brief examination of the contribution of the Vijayanagara rulers towards Vedic studies, in their role as patrons of *agrahāras* and *mathas* for the promotion of Sanskrit and Vedic education. This was an especially significant era when *mathas* grew in importance and sustained religious education, and their leaders gained immense social and ritual status. But, it was probably Sanskrit and its key role in the life and culture of the people that inspired the Vijayanagara rulers to rejuvenate and patronize Vedic studies.

It is universally accepted that Vedic literature is one of the oldest and most authentic record of the Aryans in India stretching back to the third millennium B.C. E. if not earlier. However due to the linguistic complexities of old Indo-Arya -that is Vedic Sanskrit- the language had grown to be difficult to understand due to its oral tradition. The *Vedas* were simple revelations to the *rishis* from the eternal sound waves which were divine and indestructible. Reducing these revealed texts to a set of written forms was perhaps regarded as sacrilege and was perhaps unwarranted because oral transmission was the best way to preserve the *chandas* and the contextual purity of the Vedic hymns.

By the medieval period in Indian history, there had been numerous changes in the language and grammar of Sanskrit, and the original meaning of words had been shrouded in mystery and phrases were non-comprehensible even by Sanskrit scholars. In the *Brāhmanas*, which are a part of the *Vedas,* a single word could be given different meanings because the words had changed their form, sound and meaning as well probably because the hymns were composed by different poets that spread over a vast area or perhaps due the to the long period of time taken to compose that poetry. The local dialects must have been partly used in the composition of hymns. There were innumerable difficulties that traditional commentators and translators were confronted while extracting the correct meaning of the words. Max Muller who translated the Vedas in the nineteenth century under the patronage of the East India Company considered the Vedic language to be a dead language, which was a mistake. It was the language of philosophy, religion, science and art.

Western scholars had not understood the import of many words used in the *Rigveda*. According to Bhagawan Singh, even key words like *dévata* and *rishi* have been misinterpreted by Macdonell, despite the fact that these words are defined in the *Brhaddevata*.[1] According to Sunaka, he who spoke in a dialogue is the *rishi* of that verse. He may not necessarily be a poet, but only a character, human or subhuman. Similarly, *dévata* does not mean divinity, but could be a deity, an action or an object and thus in the list of *rishis* we have Indra, Garuda and Sarpa. In the list of *dévatas* we have *ashva* or horse, *ulukhala* or pressing stone, etc. Griffith wrongly translated *samudra* as floods; on the contrary, the context clearly suggests ocean. As Macdonell misinterpreted some words, modern scholars find it difficult to make sense of many passages in the hymns.

A careful study of the *Rigveda* and other texts may throw new light on the achievements of the Vedic people, such as in the field of science and technology, trade and commerce, agriculture and industry, art and craft besides what we know about Vedic religion, philosophy, rituals, astronomy and mathematics. The meaning of these Vedic terms is substantiated by the archaeological finds from the recent excavations at Lothal, Kalinbangan and other sites.

Before we discuss the state of material civilization during the Vedic period, it is necessary to clear the misconceptions about their language and writing. It is erroneous to think that the Vedic and/or pre-Vedic period did not know the mode of scripts for their spoken language has been convincingly refuted by recent scholarship. However, it is important to understand that the rationale for the oral mode of preservation and transmission of the Vedic texts has nothing to do with the presence or absence of a script for the spoken language. The hymns of the *Rigveda* were not reduced to writing not because there was no writing during the period, but because it had not developed signs for all signs and sounds which the human voice could express. This has been used as a negative evidence by western scholars to assert that it is the Phoenicians who invented the alphabet. But discoveries in archaeological excavations at Lothal, Kalibangan, Dholavira, Bahawali, Mohenjodaro, Mehragarh and Rehman Dheri, have provided evidence of their relation with Vedic language. The recent interpretations and readings of the Harappan script on the Indus seals have clearly indicated that Indus seals shows affinity the Indo-Europena languages, such as the old Indo-Aryan or Vedic, Old Iranian including Avenstan, Old Persian and Hittite. It is closest to the language of the Rig Veda and to a limited extent to the Old Iranian and its affinity with the Hittite language is least. What is however interesting is that the basic concepts about cosmology, society and state held by the Indus and Rigvedic people is almost identical. The Indus religion acts as a link between the Vedic and Avestan faiths. This is particularly true of the fire cult of the Indus, Vedic and Iranian religions.

The fire cult of the Harappans has many parallels with the Iranian fire cult in regard to symbolism, and might have differed in ritualistic details with the Vedic fire cult, although the basic concept of fire as energy in three forms is common to Indus and Vedic cosmology. The symbol of fire cult in the Indus religion is the fire altar or fire post depicted on every seal which is engraved with a unicorn motif.

The epigraphical reference to fire god, Arka is corroborated by structural evidence too: the blazing tongues of flame are shown in the seal in three tiers symbolic of three forms of energy, namely fire, sun and lightning. The triple aspect of Agni indicated by the epithet *tridha* in the *Rigveda* finds mention several times in Indus inscriptions. The three tiered flame and the fire altar on seals symbolize the fire god and the inscription on one of the seals reads bag-bhag-rk-a-hu, conveying the sense of might or bountiful, Arka Lord. Arka stands for fire in the *Rigveda*.[2] On another seal the anthropomorphic form of Agni is shown in an arch of flame and the inscription reads bhag-rk-a= bhaga arka, lord Arka. The majority of seals carry the unicorn and fire-altar motif perhaps because either the fire worshippers were in a majority or held sway over non-fire worshippers.

A number of scholars have been researching and collecting data from Vedic texts to ascertain the progress made by Vedic Aryans in the field of agriculture, metallurgy, town planning, public hygiene, metrology and ceramics, geology, transport system, mathematics, astronomy, linguistics and altar geometry. A few technical terms relating to various on subjects occurring in the *Vedas* are noted by Bhagwan Sing, R.S. Bisht and Chattopadhyaya.[3]

Such a systematic language was often rejuvenated and patronized by kings, until the Moslem invasions. However, during the Vijayanagara period, there arose one of the most famous commentators on the *Vedas*, Sayana who revived the Vedic language to life and provided an incentive to Sanskrit scholarship, to revive religious learning and spiritual knowledge. All the four *Vedas* were translated into simple Sanskrit by a team of scholars led by Asthan Vidwan Sayanacharya. The incentive of the Vijayanagara king, Bukka Raya was noteworthy at a time when religious institutions were not stable. The group consisted of erudite scholars of Vedic Vyakarana (grammar), philosophy and Mimansa. The scholarship enabled both Indian and western scholars to understand the meaning of the hymns. It had been about five hundred years till anyone had attempted to do this. The other scholar who had undertaken the task of translating and commenting on the *Vedas*, was Yaska in his work *Nirukta* which is dated eighth to sixth centuries B.C.E or may be earlier. The *Nirukta* is considered to be one of the branches of the *Vedas*, called *Vedangas*. It consist of two parts, namely *Nirukta* and *Nighata*. In the former, text words having similar meaning are brought together while in the latter the etymology of words selected from some hymns is given along with the opinion of other *rishis*. The three main commentators on the *Rigveda* are Skandaswamy, Venkatamadhava and Sayanacharya. The commentaries by Sayana are elaborate but the interpretation is mostly from the point of view of religious practices. His *Bhashya*, which is related to the performances of *yajnas* and *yagas* (sacrifices) gives the meaning of each word and reference to earlier anecdotes and explains the meaning with reference to *Nirukta*, *vyakarana*, *chandas* and *mimamsa*.

The Sanskrit language which had been developed from such ancient times, was indeed sacred and required to be preserved by rulers who considered themselves as protectors of *dharma*. Religious traditions including art and literature were preserved in the Sanskrit language and promotion of these studies was equally important for the preservation of Hindu thought and culture.

The Vijayanagara king, Bukkaraya is said to have patronized Sayana who made a valuable contribution to Sanskrit semantics. Devaraya, ruling from

Hampi, granted the village of Satyavangala in the Marrugallunadu of Anebiddasari-sime within the *Ghanasaila maharajya* as an *agrahāra* renaming it as Devarayapura. The newly formed *agrahāra* was divided into 64 *vritis* and distributed to 47 *brāhmanas* learned in the Vedas.[4] The Vijayanagara brothers patronized numerous *agrahāras* or brahmanical villages and in fact the name of Vidyaranya was associated with an *agrahāra*. Historical evidences show that the king, Bukkaraya made donations to Bharatitirha. Harihara is said to have inherited a wealth of knowledge form Vidyaranya, who was both the *kulaguru* and *rajaguru* of the Vijayanagara kings and even the name Vijayanagara is said to have been derived from Vidyaranya.

Agrahāras were essentially centers of learning where *brāhmana* residents of the *agrahāras* were well versed in several branches of learning such as *Vedas*, *Vedangas, Sastras, Puranas*, and Logic. Here, teachers known as *upadhyaya, akkariga, bhatta, sastri, pandita, āchārya and bhattopadhyaya* were maintained with the help of royal gifts and endowments. Grants were made for the maintenance of teachers and support for students as well, and in turn, the *agrahāras* were named after the donor. For instance, the *agrahāra* Ballalapura was named after the king Viraballala.[5] Some of the important *agrahāras* in Karnataka were those in Kondaguli in Bijapur district, Kotavumachige in Gadag, Kukunur in Raichur district, Lokkigundi in Gadag, Priya Naragunda in Dharwad district, and Talagunda in Shimoga district. In Talagunda, evidences suggest that subjects such as *Rigveda, Yajurveda, Samaveda*, *Kalpa, Sabdasastra, Rupavatara, Nyasa, Prabhakara, Vedanta* and Kannada were taught here. There were forty eight students who were studying here and separate classes were conducted for different subjects.[6]

However, apart from *agrahāras*, there were *gurukulas* and *mathas* which maintained teachers and students and imparted education. The Vijayanagara rulers patronized *mathas*, in particular which had now grown important as educational institutions. Due to the changing social and political circumstances, *mathas* obtained royal grants by the kings to expand in new lands. These religious institutions were headed by gurus who were the heads of *mathas*. The power of the gurus over kings can be seen from the role of Vidyaranya in Vijayanagara. In fact, even now, in Anegondi, the present descendent of the king of Anegondi is invited to honor and crown the guru before the Virupaksha temple, before the beginning of the annual Virupakshotsava ritual ceremony. Such traditions of reverence and respect to gurus was an important factor for the growth of innumerable *mathas* in the Vijayanagara kingdom. There were Smarta *mathas*, Lingayat *mathas*, Madhva *mathas* and others which normally contained the remains of the founder guru. Mathas were institutions with an agenda and their objective was to maintain the continuity of religious and Sanskrit education, fund-raising and promotion of Vedic studies. They grew in importance and even yielded social and political power.

Thus, the institutions of learning and education, namely the *agrahāras* and *mathas*, played a key role in the rejuvenation of Hinduism and were providers of priests, chanters of mantras, scholars, scholars, saints, advisors, social reformers, teachers to kings and loyal supporters of *rājadharma*. The institutions of learning and education were rejuvenated by the Vijayanagara kings which had a lasting effect on both Sanskrit and vernacular studies in the history of South India.

Notes and References

1 Bhagwan Singh, *The Vedic Harappans (Delhi: Aditya Prakashan, 1995).*

2 S.R. Rao, *Aksaram : The Alphabet Gallery(Lipi Vethika)* (Tirupati: Rashtriya Sanskirt Vedyapeetha, 2002), 58ff.

3 D.P. Chattopadhyaya and Ravindra Kumar,ed.,*Science, Philosophy and Culture (2 parts) (Delhi: Project of History of Indian Science, Philosophy and Culture, 1996).*

4 M. V. Visweswara and D.V. Pramasiava Murthy, Satyavangala Copper Plates of Puradha Devaraya:saka 1348 in *Sri Nagabhinandanam*: ed by L.K.Srinivasan and S. Nagaraju, M.S. Nagaraja Rao Felicitation committee, 1995. pp. 614-628. Rigveda Samhita 32 Vols. (Kannada) ed. By H. Venkata Rao and others (Mysore), Griffith R.H. *The Hymns of the Rigveda.*

5 S. Leela shantakumari, *History of the Agraharas of Karnatak, 400-1300 (Madras: New Era Publidcations, 1985),26.*

6 Shantakumari, op. cit., 157

Griffith R.H., *The Hymns of the Rigveda.*

Rao, S.R., *Dawn and Devolution of the Indus Civilization.* New Delhi: Adiya Prakashan, 1991.

Rao, S.R., *The Decipherment of the Indus Script.* Bombay: Asia Publishing House, 1982.

Rao, S.R., *Lothal and the Indus Civilization.* Delhi, Asia Publishing House, 1973. Rigveda Samhita 32 Vols. (Kannada) ed. By H. Venkata Rao and others (Mysore).

9

Cosmology and Sacred Architecture in India

Subhash Kak

This paper presents the mathematical and astronomical context for the sacred architecture of India. Hindu temple art presents visions of the cosmos, which acknowledges the world of gods as existing beyond the physical plane. The temple is a sacred space that mirrors the world of the gods, in which structures repeat across space, scale, and time. The primary Vedic number is three, representing the tripartite division of the physical world into the earth, the atmosphere, and the sky and that of the person into the physical body, the *prāṇas*, and the inner sky. The temples of the Vijayanagara period, like the ones of the earlier ages, present the manifestations of the Supreme Being as the One and its many forms in a highly evolved manner. There exists, for example, a hierarchical order of cardinal and peripheral images in relation to the center, a balancing or pairing of polarities, and representation as Mount Meru, the center of the universe. The temple also served as a practical observatory where the rising sun was aligned on the equinox and solstice days with the western entrance of the temple, and many sighting lines for seasonally observing the risings of the sun and the moon. An assumed equivalence between the outer and the inner cosmos is central to the conception of the temple, and this is the basis of the connection of mathematics and astronomy to the architectural plan. It is this equivalence that makes numbers such as 108 and 360 important in temple design. The number 108 represents the approximate distance from the earth to the sun and the moon in sun and moon diameters, respectively. The diameter of the sun is also 108 times the diameter of the earth, (but that fact is not likely to have been known to the Vedic *rishis*). The physical cosmos is the template for the form of the temple and other sacred conceptions in Hinduism. The number of *karanas* or dance poses given in the *Nātyashastra* is also 108, as is the number of beads in a *japamāla* or rosary. The total number of syllables in the *Rigveda* is taken to be 432,000, a number related to 108. The number 360, the number of days in the civil year, is taken in the *Charaka Samhita* to be the number of bones in the developing foetus, a number that fuses later into the 206 bones of the adult. It will be shown how the underlying ideas of equivalence provide unifying themes as well as leave room open for innovation. This essay presents a historical background to the evolution of the temple and its connections to Vedic ideas of the cosmos, with an emphasis on the early period in which these basic ideas emerged.[1] Historic developments related to the symbolic and thematic representation of these cosmic ideas are also described.

Apart from the number 3 (tripartite division of time, space, and body), numbers that emphasize the equivalence between the inner and the outer worlds include 5 (for the number of elements and senses), 7 (openings in the head, the number of stars in the Great Bear constellation, days in quarter of the lunar month), and different astronomical numbers such as 12 (months), 27 and 28 (*nakshatras*), 30 (days of the month), 32 (27 *nakshatras* + 5 elements), 33 (28 *nakshatras* + 5 elements), and 180 (days of the half-year). These numbers and related proportions signify sacred knowledge and it is assumed that their use in architecture provides protection to the structure.

The underlying ideas of equivalence provide overarching unity while leaving room for innovation and specificity. In the transition from the Hoysala to the Vijayanagara temples, for example, soapstone is replaced by granite that leads to the building of large temples with towering *gopuras* and multiple *vimānas*. Large pillared *manḍapas* are used for ceremonies. More specific themes relate to the design of arches with *makaras* at the end and a *yāli* head at the apex.[2] The *yāli*, the protector of the temple is depicted in a variety of places, especially at the entrance and summit; it also provides yet another bridge to paradox and transformation. Arches carved in shallow relief suggest palace settings, which draw attention to deities and donors. Figures of gods and donors, which are cast in metal or represented in painted scenes, bridge the worlds of the mortals and the gods.

Although Vedic ideas permeate earliest Indian architecture, this view has not always been popular in the academic world. For example, the influential works of Coomaraswamy and Renou assumed that the beginnings of Indian architecture were to be traced to the early *Sūtra* texts that mention primitive structures.[3] For Coomaraswamy, the *Jātakas* and the Epics provided textual evidence of the plans of cities and city-gates, palaces, and huts and temples, but he glossed over the contradiction in his starting point when he acknowledged that while the Vedas make occasional reference to the cities of the *Dasyus*, it is to be observed that in the Brahmanical law books, which are very nearly, if not quite contemporary with the architectural period to be discussed below, cities are despised, and there are no ceremonies for urban life; the *Baudhāyana Dharma Sutra*, II.3.6.33, says It is impossible for one to obtain salvation, who lives in a town covered with dust.[4]

The assumption is that the Sutra texts belong to the period of the Dasyu cities, but these cities are outside the Vedic culture. But the Dasyus are themselves an Indo-Iranian people who show up as dahyu in the Iranian literature, the opposition between the Vedic people and the Dasyus is a conflict between groups with kinship relations. On the other hand, the first millennium, pre-Buddhist period of the early *Mahābhārata* with its description of cities does not have any account of inimical Dasyu kings. The only way to reconcile this seemingly contradictory situation is to suppose that the Vedic ritual texts describe events from the perspective of the priest families committed to an ideology of simplicity and renunciation, which remained dominant in subsequent times also. The Vedic world was like the age that followed, with its own complexity revealed in texts that do not deal with ritual.

Renou was also acutely aware of the limitations of his study and concluded his essay by remarking, If we rely on Vedic texts, we are in the presence of a type of a house that is extremely rudimentary, composed of an armature of posts, connected at the summit by transverse beams onto which a thatched covering is attached. The walls are woven mats. Neither stone nor brick is used.[5] But acknowledging that bricks were an essential part of the Vedic ritual as in the building of the *agnicayana* fire altar, he was forced to express doubt at his own conclusions by adding, Nothing obliges us to consider that the shelters described above were the normal type of private residence; a significant amount of the details that assist us in their reconstruction are provided by descriptions of ritual huts, the intended use of which is entirely different. And yet no other process of construction is mentioned in these sources. This appears particularly singular today, when we are able to measure (through recently discovered archaeological sources) the degree to which architectural technologies were known to certain prehistoric civilizations of northwest of India.

The sources of Renou from the *sutra* literature described temporary structures that were part of the ritual and, therefore, he had erred in taking that to represent the normal residence. The error is made particularly clear in *Atharvaveda* 9.3 where several verses speak of dismantling the rather flimsy structure, of which ritual we know from other sources, such as the *Kausikasutra* as well. Constituting a practice that continues to this day, the ritual-house is given to the priest who had officiated at the rite as part of his fee. To take this structure as an example of the typical residence is an obvious mistake, especially since such an interpretation is at variance with other evidence from the texts regarding the size and scale of the house.

Sacred Geometry in the Harappan Period

Important new evidence has emerged in the period since Coomaraswamy and Renou wrote their essays that demands revisiting our understanding of the architecture of both the early historic and the Vedic periods.[6] The Harappan cities have a grid plan, just as is recommended in the Vedic manuals. The square shape represents the heavens, where the four directions are the cardinal directions as well as the two solstices and the equinoxes of the orbit of the sun. There is also significant continuity in iconography, customs, and social organization.

A significant building in Mohenjodaro (Fig. 1 i) has a central courtyard and a symmetric arrangement of rooms in consonance with the symmetries underlying Vedic conceptions. [7] In it, every other room has a low brick platform that was apparently used for ritual. It also appears that a fire altar was placed in the courtyard. More evidence regarding fire altars comes from Lothal (Fig. 1 ii).

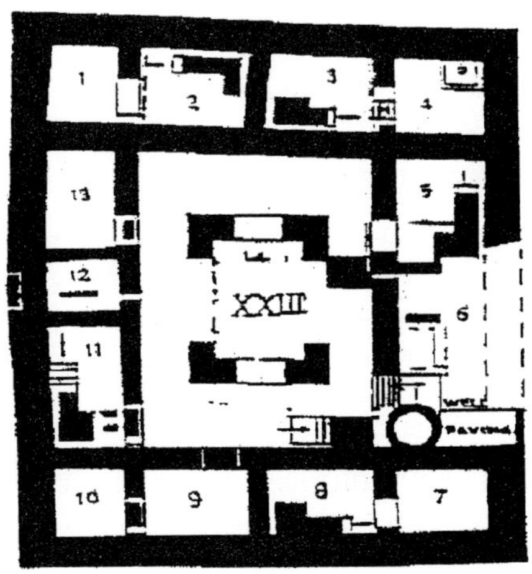

(i) Fire temple from Mohenjodaro;

Fig. 1

(ii) Fire-altar from Lothal

Fig. 1

A palace in Dashli-3 in North Afghanistan of 2000 B.C.E. (Figs. 2 and 3) uses *yāntric* forms (based on inner-outer equivalence principle) that have traditionally been considered to be late.[8] Since these forms are obviously in the Vedic tradition (although they would be correctly called post-Vedic), it is clear that palace building was a part of the tradition as early as 2000 B.C.E., if not earlier.

The *yantric* palace at Dashli-3 in North Afghanistan, 2000 BC

Fig. 2

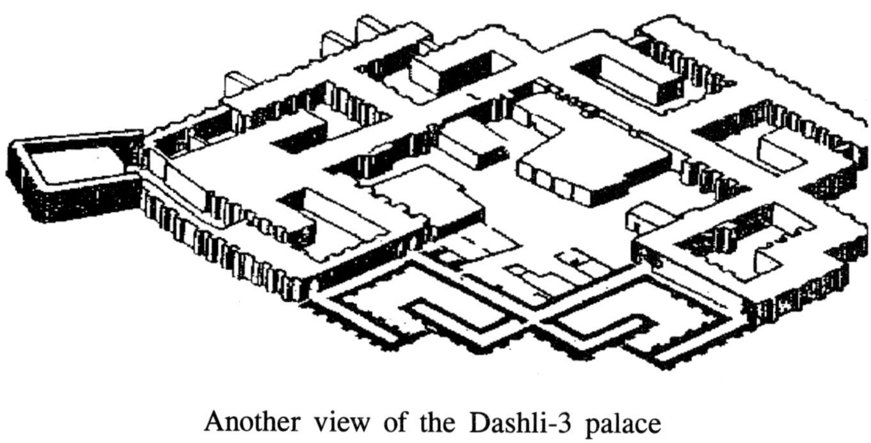

Another view of the Dashli-3 palace

Fig. 3

If one were to claim that these structures are the footprints of the immigrating Vedic people into India, one is confronted by the paradox that whereas the Vedic people knew palaces and presumably cities on their way to India, they have no memory of it when they actually arrive there. Since this is impossible, one is left with the alternative that these represent the culture of the Vedic people at a later period in their history.

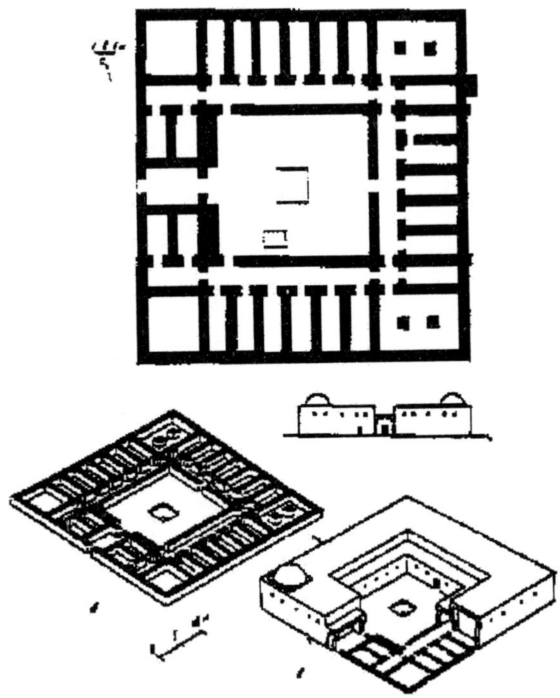

Building plan at Kutlug Tepe, Bactria c. 1st millennium B.C.E.

Fig. 4

Fig. 4 presents the building plan of a palace in Bactria dated to 1st millennium B.C.E. Its open central courtyard and the altar in the middle are remarkably similar to the plan for sacred and royal structure as provided in the *Vāstu* texts as shown in Fig. 5, confirming continuity with older ideas separated in time and space.

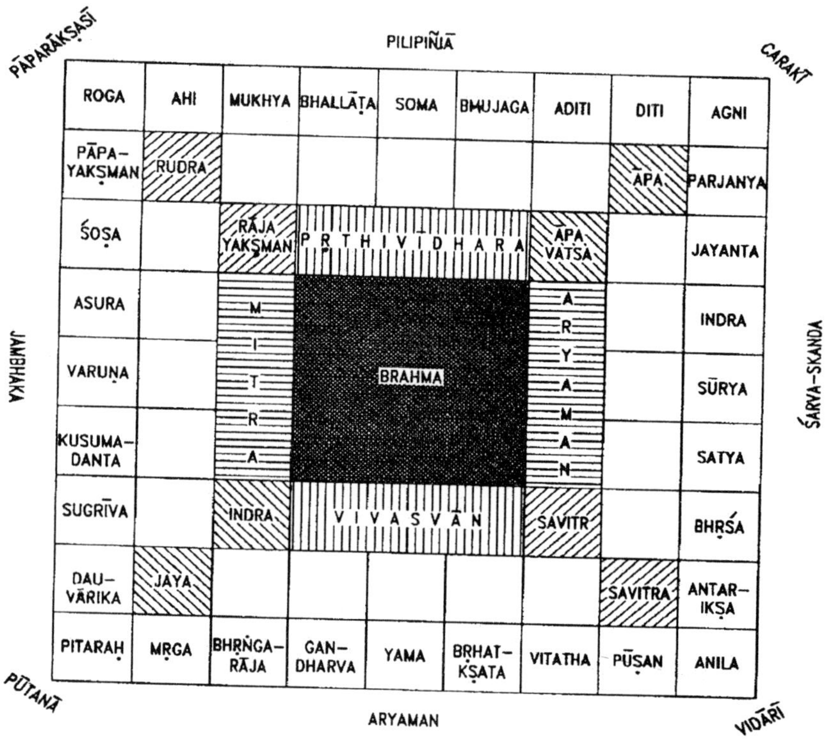

Plan for a sacred structure or house according to *Vāstu* texts

Fig. 5

The Vedic House

To understand the continuity in architectural forms, we consider the house as described in the *Rigveda*. Here is a reference to settled space as *grāma,* which is in opposition to the forest as *āranya* (RV 10.90). But within the *grāma* could be a fort or high town (*pur*). The *pur* made of stone is mentioned in *RV* 4.30.20. *Pur*s made of metal (iron) are mentioned several places such as 1.58.8, 7.3.7, 7.95.1, 10.101.8. The place of residence of the individual or joint family was *griha*, and *grāma* was a collection of *grihas*. The *dévata* presiding over each house was called *vastoshpati*. Among the many names for residence are *griham, gayah, pastyam, duronam, duryah,* *damah, okah, yonih, dhaman, niveshanam, chardis, vartih, veshman, varutham, shvaranam, vastuh, sharman, sadanam, sadas, harmyam, vidatham, guha, astam, ksayah, ama, svasram, ajman, chaya*, and so on. From a cognitive point of view, the fact of so many different names being used for a dwelling indicates a wide variety of styles and sizes.

An ordinary house with roof was *chardis* (*RV* 6.15.3); a mansion was called *harmyam,* which would have several rooms, parents, many women, and even a guard dog at the door (*RV* 1.166.4, 7.55.6, 10.55.6); and a multi-residence complex, together with halls for animals, was called *gotra*. The description of *harmyam* suggests that it had an open courtyard in the middle and quarters for women at the back. This indicates that the form was similar to the recommended plan of the later *Vāstushastra* texts. Sayana took the description in 7.55.6 to stand for a *prāsāda* or palace.

Palaces with a thousand doors and a thousand pillars are also mentioned. Renou took a similar description in RV 10.18.12 to be a metaphor, arguing, in one passage of a funerary hymn.... The poet supplicates the Earth to allow a thousand pillars to be raised in the cavity where the dead repose, so that her weight will not crush those who take refuge in her breast.[9] However, such a plausible explanation does not work for the reference to such large palaces in *RV*2.41.5, 5.62.6, 7.88.5. There is clear reference to a house that is substantial, where several families reside and which has a dog guarding it.

The house could be of many sizes, with two, four, six, eight, or ten wings. (*RV*.9.3.21). The house is said to be the home of Soma (*RV*.9.3.19); it adjusts itself to all just like a new bride adjusts to the members of the (large) family. The Vedic poets viewed a house not merely as an inanimate block of sand and grass, but as a living entity. The divinity associated with the house is addressed in (3.12.5), Lady of the mansion, our shelter, kind Goddess you were first fixed by the *devas*: May you, robed in grass, be gracious to us, and give us heroes and wealth. The house consecration ceremony described in this hymn is similar to the one done even today in Hindu families on entering a new home.

Vedic Altars and Temple Antecedents

Vedic altars had an astronomical basis related to the reconciliation of the lunar and solar years. The fire altars symbolized the universe and there were three types of altars representing the earth, the space and the sky. The altar for the earth was is circular, whereas the sky (or heaven) altar is drawn as square (Fig. 6). The geometric problems of circulature of a square and that of squaring a circle are a result of equating the earth and the sky altars.

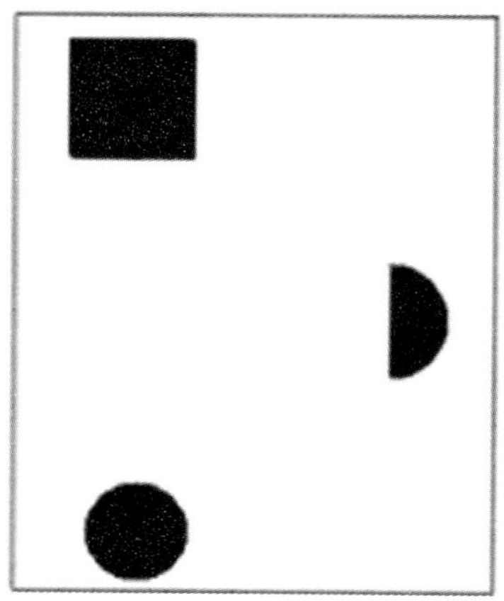

Three basic Vedic altars

Fig. 6

The fire altars were surrounded by 360 enclosing stones, of these 21 were around the earth altar, 78 around the space altar and 261 around the sky altar. In other words, the earth, the space, and the sky are symbolically assigned the numbers 21, 78, and 261. Considering the earth/cosmos dichotomy, the two numbers are 21 and 339 since cosmos includes the space and the sky. The main altar was built in five layers. The basic square shape was modified to several forms, such as falcon and turtle. These altars were built in five layers, of a thousand bricks of specified shapes. The construction of these altars required the solution to several geometric and algebraic problems.

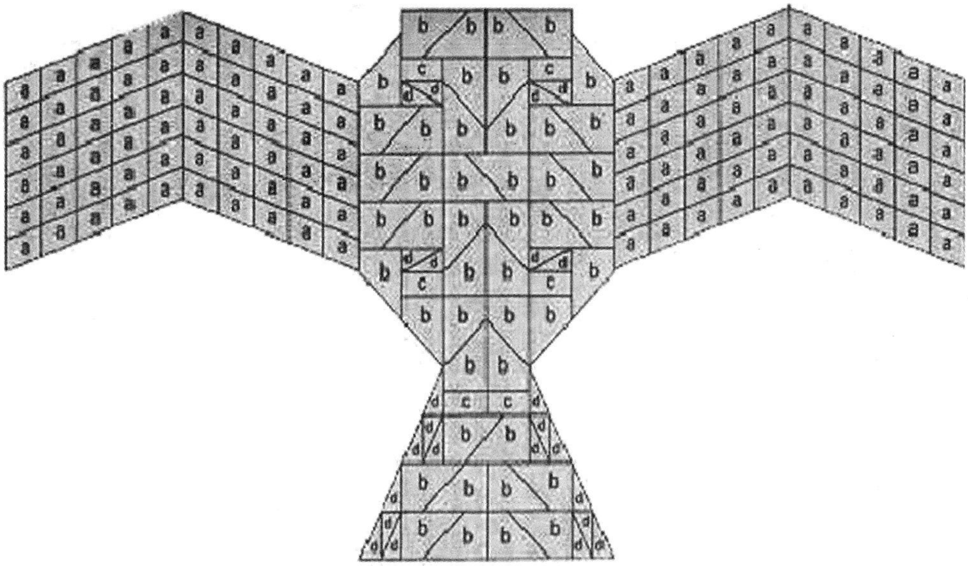

The falcon altar

Fig. 7

Two different kinds of bricks were used: the special and the ordinary. The total number of the special bricks used was 396, explained as 360 days of the year and the additional 36 days of the intercalary month. Two kinds of day counts: the solar day, and *tithi*, whose mean value is the lunar year divided into 360 parts. Considering the altar by layers, the first has 98, the second has 41, the third has 71, the fourth has 47 and the fifth has 138. The sum of the bricks in the fourth and the fifth layers equals 186 *tithis* of the half-year. The number of bricks in the third and the fourth layers equals the integer nearest to one third the number of days in the lunar year, and the number of bricks in the third layer equals the integer nearest to one fifth of the number of days in the lunar year, and so on.

The number of ordinary bricks equals 10,800 which equals the number of *muhurtas* in a year (1 day = 30 *muhurtas*), or equivalently the number of days in 30 years. Of these 21 go into the *gārhapatya*, 78 into the eight *dhisnya* hearths, and the rest go into the *āhavaniya* altar. The main altar was an area of 7 1/2 units. This area was taken to be equivalent to the nominal year of 360 days. Each subsequent year, the shape was to be reproduced with the area increased by one unit.

Three different years were considered: (i) *nakshatra,* or a year of 324 days (sometimes 324 *tithis*) obtained by considering 12 months of 27 days each, where this 27 is the ideal number of days in a lunar month; (ii) lunar, which is a fraction more than 354 days (360 *tithis*); and (iii) *solar,* which is in excess of 365 days (between 371 and 372 *tithis*). A well-known altar ritual says that altars should be constructed in a sequence of 95, with progressively increasing areas. The increase in the area, by one unit yearly, in building progressively larger fire altars is 48 *tithis* which is about equal to the intercalation required to make the *nakshatra* year in *tithis* equal to the solar year in *tithis*. But there is a residual excess which in 95 years adds up to 89 *tithis*; it appears that after this period such a correction was made. The 95 year cycle corresponds to the tropical year being equal to 365.24675 days. The cycles needed to harmonize various motions led to the concept of increasing periods and world ages.

The number of syllables in the R*igveda* confirms the textual references that the book was to represent a symbolic altar. The verse count of the *Rigveda* can be viewed as the number of sky days in forty years or 261 ṅ 40 = 10,440, and the verse count of all the *Vedas* is 261 ṅ 78 = 20,358. The *Brāhmanas* tell us about the altar of *chandas* and meters, so we would expect that the total Rigvedic hymn count of 1017 and the group count of 216 have particular significance. Owing to the pervasive tripartite ideology of the Vedic books we choose to view the hymn number as 339 x 3. The tripartite ideology refers to the consideration of time in three divisions of past, present, and future and the consideration of space in the three divisions of the northern celestial hemisphere, the plane that is at right angle to the earth's axis, and the southern celestial hemisphere. The number 339 is simply the number of disks of the sun or the moon to measure the path across the sky: p times 108 is approximately 339. The number 216 is the distance to the sky, which is twice the distance of 108 to the sun. The

Rigvedic code then expresses a fundamental connection between the numbers 339 and 108.

The prototype of the temple is the *agnikshetra,* the sacred ground on which the Vedic altars are built. The *agnikshetra* is an oblong or trapezoidal area on which the fire altars are built. Tripathi has argued[11] that the *agnicayana* sacred ground provides the prototype, because in it is installed a golden disc (*rukma*) with 21 knobs or hangings representing the sun with a golden image of the *purusha* on it. Tripathi shows that the detailed ritual includes components that would now be termed Shaiva, Vaishnava, or Shakta. In Naciketa Agni, 21 bricks of gold are placed one top of the other in a form of Shiva *linga*. The disk of the *rukma,* which is placed in the navel of the altar on a lotus leaf is in correspondence to the lotus emanating from Vishnu's navel which holds the universe. Several bricks are named after goddesses, such as the seven *krttikas*. The temple is the representation of the cosmos both at the level of the universe and the individual, making it possible for the devotee to get inspired to achieve his own spiritual transformation. The *purusha* placed within the brick structure of the altar represents the consciousness principle within the individual. It is like the relic within the *stupa*.

Complementing the tradition of the Vedic ritual was that of the *munis* and yogis who lived in caves and performed austerities. From this tradition arose the *vihara*, where the priests lived. The *chaitya* hall that also housed the *stupa,* may be seen as a development out of the *agnicayana* tradition where within the brick structure of the altar were buried the *rukma* and the golden man (see *Shatapatha Brahmana* 7.4.1 for details; 7.4.2 describes how above the man is placed a perforated brick which encases it like a casket). There were two innovations at the end of the Vedic period: the use of stone to build sacred structures that were originally built of brick or wood, and representation of cosmic ideas in terms of paradox-rich iconography associated with divinity.

The classical temple construction begins with the *vāstupurushamanḍala* which is a *yantra*, mostly divided into 64 (8 ṅ 8) or 81 (9 ṅ 9) squares, which are the seats of 45 divinities. *Brahma* is at the centre, around him 12 squares represent the *adityas*, and in the outer circle are 28 squares that represent the *nakshatras* (Fig. 5). The *vastumandala* with its border is the place where the motions of the sun and the moon and the planets are reconciled. It is the *vāstu* in which the decrepit, old *Cyavana* of the *Rigveda* 1.116.10 asks his sons to put him down so that he would become young again. *Cyavana* is the moon and *Sukanya*, whom he desires, is the sun.

The altar or the temple, as a representation of the dynamism of the universe, requires a breaking of the symmetry of the square. In the *agnicayana* and other altar constructions, this is done in a variety of ways. Although the main altar might be square or its derivative, the overall sacred area is taken to be a departure from this shape. In particular, the temples to the goddess are drawn on a rectangular plan. In Shiva or Vishnu temples, which are square, change is represented by a play of diagonal lines. These diagonals are essentially kinetic and are therefore representative of movement and stress. They embody the time-factor in a composition. The progressive complexity of the classical temple was inevitable given an attempt to bring in the cycles of the planets and other ideas of the *yugas* into the scheme. Further complexity was related to the representation of the *tattvas* within the temple, as well as the fundamental Vedic notions of paradox and transformation.

Movement and Image

Vedic models of the cosmos in terms of abstract relationships in the fire altars were enlarged in the *Nirukta* by Yaska (eighth century B.C.E.?) and the *Ashtadhyayi* of Panini (fifth or fourth century B.C.E.) mentions images.[12] Ordinary images were called *pratikrti* and the images for worship were called *arca*. Amongst other things we are told that a toy horse is called *ashvaka*.[13] Deity images for sale were called Shivaka etc., but an *arca* of Shiva was just called Shiva. Patanjali mentions Shiva and Skanda deities. There is also mention of the worship of Vasudeva (Krishna). We are also told that some images could be moved and some were immoveable. Panini also says that an *arca* was not to be sold and that there were people (priests) who obtained their livelihood by taking care of it. They also mention temples that were called *prāsādas*. *Vāstu* texts, which present the temple plan as homological to a human body. The human body serves as the plan for all creation as in the *purushasukta*. The temple structure is homologous to the standing *purusha* as the *shilpa-paüjara*. At a lower level, a similar measure informs the proportions of the sculpted form, that may be standing or seated, and also of painted figures. This body at its deepest level is a body of knowledge. The structure of music is also to be conceived as such a body; hence one can speak of the *sangitapurusha*, where there exist precise relationships between ascending and descending notes.

From the central point of the *garbhagriha*, there proceeds expansion in all directions of space, reaching to the *bindu* above the finial of the temple and beyond. The temple may be equivalently be seen as a manifestation held together by tension between the *bindu* and the *garbhagriha*, with the axis joining the two being the world axis. Typically, the temple has a stone or brick structure, which is in the image of a wooden building. Where it is too difficult or expensive to construct a stone or masonry temple, it may be built of wood or any other available material. The idea behind use of stone, but in the image of wood ṭ normally the building material for the residential house is to project that the wooden, or human, nature of the conception is to find expression in the much more permanent stone just as the transcendent category of divinity is given the iconic expression derived from the human world.[15]

There is also the question of the details of the superstructure, and we see repeated forms and motifs, to different scales. This represents the fundamental Vedic idea of recursion in reality. The recursion is also seen in exterior decoration and composition and its basic compositional elements and grammar related to the joining of these elements has been described in the texts. The temple, together with its images, represents movement and change. This is achieved by the use of projection, extension and repetition across different scales. An extension at the center of the body of the form is a *bhadra*; when located at the corner, it is a *karma;* located between the *bhadra* and the corner, it is a *pratibhadra*. Their use in different ways creates unique representations out of the basic *vastupurushamanḍala*.

Movement is also expressed by increasingly concrete representation of an image, from *nishkala* to *sakala*.[16] To illustrate the last idea, the emanations of Shiva are in the form of a formless *linga* as the axis of materiality and consciousness (*nishkala*), to the intermediate *nishkala-sakalamukhalinga* which has faces in cardinal directions (Sadashiiva), to the *sakalamahesha* (the anthropomorphic Shiva). There are also other variations: Shiva with one face and two hands, or with four hands; Shiva with four, five, eight, or twelve faces; Shiva with bull, lion, or elephant; Shiva and Parvati; Ardhnarishvara, Harihara, Dakshinamurti, and Aja-Ekapad. The faces emerging out of the plain *linga*, along the cardinal directions, are those of *Sadyojta, Aghora, Tatpurusha, and Vamadeva*. For *Mahesha*, the corresponding emanations are Shiva, Vishnu, Surya, and Brahma.

Shiva inheres in himself all contradictions, just as is the case with our reality. He grants wealth and prosperity but is himself clad in elephant hide and he is a beggar; he is personification of asceticism, yet half of his body is that of his consort. Shiva manifests in different forms: as *vishvarupa* or the universe, as *lingasharira* in the hearts of beings, and as the omnipresent *antaratman* in the heart of all beings. Shiva is Maheshvara, the great Lord, Mahadeva, the great God, and Mrtyunjaya, conqueror of death. He is the spouse of Shakti, the Goddess and a yogin. His usual mantra is *Om namah Shivaya*. When symbolized as the Sun at dawn in conjunction with the moon, he is shown with matted locks with the crescent moon, from which streams the river Ganga, symbolic of the Milky Way. He is smeared with ash, symbolizing all that remains at the dissolution of the universe. This dissolution occurs when his third eye opens, which refers to our symbolic death and renewal with the realization of our consciousness. His right hand shows the *mudra* dispelling fear, while in his left he holds the trident, symbol of the three worlds, on which is bound the *damaru*.

Vishnu's *trivikram,* the three steps that measure out the universe, represent the order in change (*vikrama*) that binds the three worlds of the outer, the inner, and the elements. Vishnu is God in its moral embodiment, represented by word and form, whereas Shiva is the inner core of reality. Vishnu is the universe, Shiva is its axis. The dichotomy of the phenomenal world may be seen through the lens of ongoing change associated with Nature, *prakriti*. According to the T*antras*, transcendent reality manifests itself in to the pair Shiva and Shakti. Shiva, paradoxically, is the cause of bondage; Shakti the force of liberation. The Goddess is the life force of the universe. She is represented by the vowel *i* in the name of Shiva; without it Shiva is *shava*, a dead body. In Shaivite temples, the *linga* is generally placed before an image of his *vāhana* or vehicle, Nandi, the bull.

Concluding Remarks

This essay has provided a brief history of representation of outer and inner cosmos in the sacred architecture of the Vedic tradition. The outer cosmos is symbolized by various astronomical connections between the temple structure and the motions of the sun, the moon, and the planets; the inner cosmos is represented by the deity in the womb of the temple. The various levels of the superstructure correspond to different layers of outer and inner cosmos. Astronomy of the Vedic altars provides clues to the understanding of the cosmology that has continued to play a central role in the sacred architecture of India in both the Hindu and the Buddhist traditions.

The position of the gods in the *vastupurushamandala* within the temple is a symbolic representation of the spatial projections of the cosmic *purusha*. There are other iconic representations of sacred space, as in the *Shri Yantra* where the three parts of the body - *vagbhava*, *madhya* and *mula* - have recursive structures within, leading to the 43 triangles of the design, that represent Vedic cosmology in a unique fashion. The articulation of the knowledge in terms of numerical proportions as well as mythological narrative endowed the structure with auspiciousness and power.

The classical temple, consistent with the cosmology of the Vedic text, evolved as an enlargement of ideas of equivalence through several devices of numerical representation and pictorial narrative, as is most clear in the great

Hindu temples of India and Southeast Asia, which bridged the worlds of gods and men. Thus the Brihadeshvara temple depicts the 108 dance poses of Shiva. The inverted shadow of the eastern tower at Virupaksha or the Pampapati temple at Hampi falls on the western wall through a small hole behind the sanctum. The manifestations of Shiva, and the incarnations of Vishnu are portrayed here, as is the classic scene from *Mahabharata* depicting Arjuna, shooting of the fish device in order to secure the hand of Draupadi in marriage. There is also a mural depicting Vidyaranya the spiritual founder of Vijayanagara in procession. The Vijayanagara temples were founded on cosmic and symbolic cosmology which were deeply rooted in the Vedic tradition.

Notes and Reference

1 S. Kak, *The Architecture of Knowledge* (Delhi: CRC/Motilal Banarsidass, 2004); Kak, *The Gods Within* (New Delhi:Munshiram Manoharlal, 2002).

2 M.W. Meister ed., *Encyclopaedia of Indian Temple Architecture.* Vol. 1, pt 1, *South India, Lower Dravidadesa* (New Delhi: AIIS, 1983); M.W. Meister.ed., *Discourses on Siva* (Philadelphia: University of Pennsylvania Press, 1984); G. Michell, *Architecture and Art of Southern India* (Cambridge: Cambridge University Press,1995); A. Hardy, *Indian Temple Architecture: Form and Transformation* (New Delhi: Indira Gandhi National Centre for the Arts and Abhinav Publications, 1995).

3 This material has been reprinted and is available as Ananda K. Coomaraswamy, *Essays in Early Indian Architecture* (Delhi: Indira Kalakendra and Oxford University Press, 1992) and Louis Renou, The Vedic house in *Res*, 34, 143-161, 1998, both edited by Michael W. Meister.

4 Coomaraswamy, *Essays in Early Indian Architecture*, 3.

5 Renou, *op. cit.,*160-1.

6 S.R. Rao, *Dawn and Devolution of the Indus Civilization* (New Delhi: Aditya Prakashan, 1991); B.B. Lal, *The Earliest Civilization of South Asia.* (Delhi: Aryan Books International, 1997).

7 M.K. Dhavalikar and Shubhangana Atre, The fire cult and virgin sacrifice: some Harappan rituals, in *Old Problems and New Perspectives in the*

Archaeology of South Asia, J.M. Kenoyer , ed. (Dept of Anthropology, University of Wisconsin, 1989), 193-205.

8 V.I. Sarianidi, *Drevnie zemeldeltsy Afganistana*. Moskva, 1977. For a contextualized discussion of this structure, see S. Kak, *The Astronomical Code of the Rigveda* (New Delhi: Munshiram Manoharlal, 2000).

9 Renou, *op cit*, Section 18, page 157.

10 S. Kramrisch, *The Presence of Siva* (Princeton University Press, 1992); B.U. Nayak and N.C. Ghosh, ed. *New Trends in Indian Art and Archaeology* (New Delhhi: Aditya Prakashan, 1992); S. Kak, Ritual, Masks, and Sacrifice in *Studies in Humanities and Social Sciences*, IIAS Simla, vol. 11, 2004, 29-44.

11 V. Tripathi, *Agnicayana* (Varanasi: Sampurnanand Sanskrit University, 1990).

12 T.A. Gopinatha Rao, *Elements of Hindu Iconography*. 1872-1919. Reprinted (New York: Garland Publishing, 1981).

13 This means that the queen who lay down with the *ashvaka* in the Asvamedha did not sleep with the dead horse; see also, S. Kak, *The Asvamedha*. (Delhi: Motilal Banarsidass, 2002).

14 S. Huntington, *The Art of Ancient India*. (Weatherhill, New York, 1985).

15 S. Kak, *L'Arbre a Souhaits - Presence et Promesse de l'Inde.* Editions (Banyan: Paris, 2004).

16 D. Desai, Manifestation of order in art: the iconic scheme at Khajuraho, In *Rta: The Cosmic Order*. Khanna, M. ed. (New Delhi: D.K. Printworld, 2004); see also, R. Kaulacara, *Silpa Prakasa.* Boner, A. and Rath Sarma, S. eds. (Leiden: E.J. Brill, 1966); A. Boner, A., 1962. *Principles of Composition in Hindu Sculpture* (E.J. Brill, Leiden, 1962; A. Volwahsen, *Cosmic Architecture in India.* (New York: Prestel, and Mapin Publishing, 2001).

10

Cultural Heritage Planning of Sacred Sites: A Case Study of Rockfort Temple at Tiruchirapalli, India

Aparna Raghnathan and Amita Sinha

The article presents a case study of a sacred site in India, Rockfort Temple Complex at Tiruchirapalli, Tamil Nadu. A group of excavated and structural temples are located on a hill on the banks of the river Kaveri surrounded by a medieval fort that became the nucleus of urban growth over time. Restoring and developing this richly layered and complex site with its ever-increasing numbers of pilgrims is a challenge.

Overwhelming growth of commerce within the last half century has resulted in many problems such as traffic congestion, confusing circulation, and visual chaos, which in turn have led to the loss of sacred ambience. We propose that conservation of sacred landscape become an urban planning and design tool. The structure of the pilgrim landscape constituted by circumambulatory paths, tanks and groves, shrines and temples can be clarified and made legible by minor design interventions such as restoring historic buildings, reviving the holy tanks, planting sacred trees, and building rest pavilions along the pilgrim path.

While architectural heritage is the subject of many preservation and conservation efforts in India, historic and cultural landscapes have received little attention in this regard. Sacred sites, hallowed by mythology and living traditions, embody the true heritage of India. Often these sites have also been historically seats of royal power due to the belief in their ability to ensure moral order. Thus there is a rich legacy of natural and built heritage at these places although unfortunately only the latter receives any institutional protection. Historic buildings at World Heritage Sites in South India such as Hampi, Pattadakal, Brihideshvara temple at Thanjavur, and Mahabalipuram are well preserved but it is spaces between and around them that need to be developed as part of archaeological parks or cultural heritage districts so that the visual and physical connections in the past between buildings and landscape are restored. Other pilgrim sites such as temple towns that are vibrant, thriving places of worship also require careful management of the physical landscape and appropriate development of amenities for the large number of their visitors.

Natural and Spatial Archetypes

Conservation of sacred sites should be based upon an understanding of forms and their meanings that constitute the traditional vocabulary of their landscapes. These cultural landscapes, created from the natural world, and shaped by human actions, have natural and spatial archetypes as their building blocks. We use the word Archetype in the Jungian sense, as psychic nodes manifested in psychic symbols, natural elements and spatial patterns. These symbols are physical manifestation of concepts that have held a central position with the cultural corpus of Indic religions, and as such are capable of conveying profound meanings.

In nature are found archetypal forms that have inspired human creation since the beginning of time and have thus become the loci of meanings projected by the human mind. Natural elements – mountains, caves, water, vegetation, and their combination hold the potential for becoming *axis mundi*, center of the known world, where communication with the non-human and godly realms is possible. The river Ganga, the Mount Kailash, and the Bodhi Tree are examples of visible axes between the earth, the heavens and the underworld. They play a crucial role in cultural narratives of mythology and are represented in art and literature as cultural icons. Mountains, rivers, and trees found in different parts of the subcontinent are named after them. Every sacred site has a prominent natural feature, whether it is a hill, river, forest grove, or a combination of all three.

In contrast to pre-existing natural archetypes, spatial archetypes are a human creation, forming the basis of spatial organization of settlements and buildings. They have their origin in the perception of sacred sites as *bhu-mandalas*, reinforced through ritual circumambulations by pilgrims around natural features. Space is generated, physically and cognitively, by this act of inscription in the landscape. It is created from movement around a center, orientation to cardinal directions, and delimitation of sacred zone from profane. It is given shape in the spatial archetype of *mandala* that is endowed with great meaning and read metonymically as a symbol of the cosmos. Temples erected to house deities and facilitate worship are based upon the *vāstupurushamandala*.

The focus of conservation planning and design efforts in sacred sites should be on their landscape heritage in which natural and spatial archetypal forms are primary components, interwoven in a complex ensemble. All of these sites, originally selected or discovered for their spectacular natural features, have been built and rebuilt over the ages with a consistent vocabulary of spatial forms. Stepped tanks, circumambulatory pathways and threshold gateways surround or are interspersed with an array of temples, small and large. To accommodate increasing human use, the natural landscape gives way to a built one in which natural elements are abstracted into manmade structures. The natural setting, often hilly terrain close to river confluences, may be the only clue to the original significance of nature in the establishment of the sacred site.

In peninsular India, as in other parts of the subcontinent, sites of worship were natural settings that saw their primeval local gods and goddesses give way or co-opted over time into Brahmanical Hinduism. The banks and the delta of the river Kaveri, revered as the Southern Ganga, are dotted with pilgrim cities such as Chidambaram, Kumbakonam, Tanjavur and Tiruchirapalli that grew out of temple complexes built by the Cholas at the end of the first millennium. Besides the river body, there are other natural archetypes that were responsible for the reverence of the site as settings for or as players in mythic events. River confluences are favored sites, for example, Kanchipuram is located on the banks of the Vagavati River before it joins the Palar River flowing eastward into the Bay of Bengal. Kumbakonam is located at the banks of Kaveri where it is joined by the River Arasalar and is known as Kashi on the Kaveri. Similarly islands hold a special sanctity as they symbolize land rising out of the primeval watery chaos. The Ranganatha temple is situated in Shrirangam Island in the River Kaveri and its branch Shivagangai. The famous Venkateshwara Temple is built on the summit of Tirupati Hill on the southern banks of Pushkarini River. The 800 m high sacred hill of Tiruvannamalai is regarded as the embodiment of Shiva, who is manifested as a column of fire on its summit on Shivaratri. Chidambaram, where the ether *linga* is worshipped, was originally the Tillai forest, inhabited by Kali, whom Shiva defeated in a dance competition. Similarly the holy city of Madurai on the banks of the River Vaigai was the Kadambavanam Forest in the beginning where Indra, the king of gods, worshipped *Swayambhulingam* (self-manifested *linga, aniconic* form of Shiva) under the Kadamba Tree.

The transformation of the natural landscape of sacred sites into a monumental and urban landscape of temple towns and cities occurred over time with royal patronage. Spatial archetypes, especially the *mandala*, had a vital role to play in this evolutionary transformation of the landscape. The *mandala*, of square/rectangular concentric form, guided the growth of temple complexes with walls and *gopurams* or gateways added at increasing distances from the main central shrine, enclosing it on all four sides. This form is symbolic of cosmos as the *Puranas* (texts on myths) conceived it, in which the center – Mount Meru – is surrounded by rings of six oceans and seven continents. The built form of the temple complex thus metonymically represents the entire cosmos, in the process concentrating its auspicious energies in a defined area. The *garbhagriha* or the womb house of the main shrine is the mountain cave, the soaring towers of the *gopurams* are symbolic of mountain peaks, the oceans are represented by stepped water tanks, and the forest groves are reproduced in the pillared halls of the *mandapas*.

Often in temple towns, the *mandala* extends into the urban landscape, with the streets paralleling the temple enclosure walls. From its central shrine, the point of concentrated holiness, spread outward the munificent energies, ordering and regulating the larger landscape. The innermost enclosures are the holiest, in the outer enclosures ordinary living creeps in the residences of priestly families as does public life, created by visiting throngs of pilgrims. This landscape is experienced in ritual movement of circumambulations around the shrines as well as unidirectional approach along the main axes, threaded by multiple thresholds of sanctity represented by *gopurams*. These patterns of movement are reminiscent of circumambulations around natural features, whether they be mountains, trees or water bodies; ascension to the summit of the mountain, or penetration into the cave or the depths of the forest.

The entire cultural landscape of temple complexes including their broader regional context, therefore should be considered in drawing up planning and management guidelines for conservation. Natural and spatial archetypes interwoven in an intricate tapestry constitute the fabric of this cultural landscape. When this formal vocabulary is deciphered and understood, restoring and conserving what at first appears to be an eclectic and confusing landscape, is easier. Using the Rockfort Temple at Tiruchirapalli as a case study, we present a conceptual approach towards conservation of both natural and built landscape heritage of temple sites in South India.

Rockfort Temple in Tiruchirapalli

Of the many temples that Tiruchirapalli is famous for, the Rockfort Temple Complex on the 83 m high hillock on the banks of the river Kaveri is the city's icon, looming as it does over the urban settlement below. Although lesser known than the spectacular Shrirangam temple of seven enclosures and gigantic *gopurams* or the adjoining Jambukeshvara temple in the nearby island setting, it is visited by over 40,000 pilgrims annually. What makes it interesting is its archaic association with autochthonous mother goddess and snake cult worship, evident even now in the many *Amman* (mother goddess) shrines and *Nagakals* (stone slabs with the motif of entwined snakes) located in its vicinity and visited mostly by non-Brahmins. Within the rubric of Brahmanical Hinduism, the hillock is perceived to be the Dakshina (south) Kailash Mountain, as Kaveri is the southern Ganga.

This holy mountain-river dyad of Kailash-Ganga, the most sacred combination in Hinduism, is the perfect abode of Shiva and it is not surprising that the Lalitankura Pallaveshvaram cave temple dedicated to him, was excavated by Pallava ruler Mahendravarman in the seventh century. Its most famous sculptural panel depicts Shiva receiving the Ganga on his head, with goddess Parvati at his side. Another cave temple was excavated lower down, in the eighth century by the Pandyan rulers. From the early beginnings of excavated temples to structural temples first built by the Cholas in the tenth century and later rebuilt by the Nayaka rulers of Madurai in the sixteenth and seventeenth centuries, the hillock continued to be a sacred site and abode of Shiva, Parvati, and their son Ganesh. Presently the four most visited temples at three levels are Manikka Vinayakar (Ganesh) temple at the foot of the hill, Thayumanavar Koyil Shivasthalam (Shiva) and Matturvarkuzhal Ammai (Parvati) temples towards the west, and Ucchipillayar Temple (Ganesh) Temple on the summit on the eastern side.[1]

The temples, excavated and structural, were part of the larger cultural landscape whose basic vocabulary consisted of archetypal forms. These included sacred tanks (Teppakulam and Umayankulam), sacred grove with a shrine to the vehicle of Shiva, Nandi (Nandi Kovil), *gopurams*, circumambulatory and axial pathways going around and up the hill, and *mandapas* lining the edges of tanks and pilgrim paths. The traditional settlement of the *agrahāras* of Brahmins, consisting of a linear pattern of courtyard housing, clustered around the hill. The visually prominent hillock on the banks of the river also invited fort building, serving secular purposes of a defensive establishment. The Cholas had built their citadel at Uraiyur close by but it was the Nayakas who responsible for enclosing the temples on the hill in a fort complex as the site witnessed conflict and desecration by Islamic forces in the fourteenth century.

Although the hilly topography prevented the large scale building of concentric enclosures as at nearby Shrirangam and Jambukesvara temple complexes, the inner and outer fort walls enclosed the temple sites on the hill in a similar manner.

Urban Landscape of Rockfort

Brought under Vijayanagara rulers, the religious monuments were repaired and consecrated again for worship. As the Vijayanagara empire vanished, control passed into the hands of the Nayaks of Madurai who were followed by the Arcot Nawabs, the Marathas, Nizam of Hyderabad, the Carnatic rulers and finally the British who built a cantonment and brought the railways to Tiruchirapalli. The city experienced a huge growth in the last two centuries and became well known for its handloom cloth, glass bangles, wooden and clay toys, and jewelry. The fort walls were leveled and the moat filled up and paved over in the nineteenth century as the Municipal Works established by the British sought to improve public hygiene. The spire of churches and a bell tower, and dome of a mosque punctuated the skyline even as temples on the hill, the most visible feature of the town, continued to be the venue of local and regional pilgrimage (Fig. 1).[2]

The fort area within the city is the historic core in addition to being the sacred center. Its commercial role, however, seems to be taking over its more exalted function as a custodian of cultural heritage. Its major streets, the boulevards that replaced the moat and those leading up to them, are replete with bazaars selling a variety of merchandise, from local handicrafts to smuggled goods. As a result the roads are clogged with vehicular and pedestrian traffic, street vendors and hawkers, and parked vehicles. Billboards and fluorescent neon signs above the shops create a visual cacophony that is incongruous with *gopuram* detailing on the street from where the pilgrims begin their upward climb (Fig. 2). The most egregious obfuscation is of the sacred hill itself and its temples by four storied buildings on that street. About seventy percent of the visitors to fort area come for shopping alone. While commerce has always been a part and parcel of life in temple towns, the bazaar streets of the fort area and the crowds they bring threaten to engulf and dominate the sacred center and its associated activities.

In this overcrowded and somewhat chaotic urban environment, open spaces, particularly green areas, are scarce. Those that do remain are the historic tanks Teppakulam and Umayankulam (with a coconut grove in its vicinity), the temple garden Nandavanam with a small sacred tank, and another tank and grove around Nandi Kovil Temple. Teppakulam is a significant sacred place of gathering where the idol of Ganesha is brought during the float festival when oil lamps are lit covering the tank. Presently it is surrounded by a metallic fence with restricted access for boating, greatly diminishing the effect that would have been created by the water body surrounded by *mandapams* and sacred groves (Fig. 3).

The pilgrim path has suffered the greatest loss in its sacred ambience. In the past, the journey of the devotee to the temples would have been through a calm and quiet natural landscape. Today if she wishes to meditate, reflect, and chant her mantras as she walks from the fort gate to the *gopuram* entry, her concentration would be broken by the screaming vendors, hassling by the hawkers, and honking of cars, autorickshaws, and motorcycles, as she pushes her away through the crowd. This reduction and containment of nature as a relic of the past with increasing urbanization has been detrimental to the pilgrim experience and in a larger sense, also meant a loss of environmental and cultural heritage.

Rockfort Cultural Heritage District – An Integrated Conservation Approach

The cave temples are protected and preserved by the Archaeological Survey of India, and the popularity and ever-increasing visitation of structural temples ensures that they will be periodically renovated by the Temple Trust. But there is no understanding, let alone protection, of the larger cultural landscape of which the temples are the most significant part. It is not surprising why this is the case. Often the pressures of development are too strong to be resisted, meeting as they do the immediate and pressing needs of housing and commerce. Lack of preservation regulations has meant absence of legal enforcement of the desired course of action. Ownership in the public domain is distributed between different organizations that have to co-ordinate and reach a consensus on the conservation blueprint. Landscape heritage conservation of sacred sites therefore is an urgent necessity, requiring a legal and an administrative infrastructure that is lacking at the moment but can be easily developed.

The monument-centric approach by ASI to conservation limits efforts to only building protection and preservation, neglecting the crucial relationships that tie them with their context. An integrated conservation approach on the other hand would not only be mindful of the larger setting but also take into account the inevitable urban change and development that occurs with time.[3] In Rockfort complex, lack of legibility, confusing circulation, traffic congestion, overcrowding and lack of open spaces need immediate attention. Most importantly the loss of sacred landscapes from which the temples originally derived their meaning and that shaped the experience of pilgrimage in the past, should be reversed.

Urban conservation entails that the temples on the hill and other heritage buildings at its foot be protected and protected not as isolated structures but as part of a larger cultural heritage district that encompasses the historic Rockfort area. The boundaries of this district would be the streets that surround the hill and were built over the moat in the colonial era (Fig. 4). The area would thus be a protected zone and master plan for conservation that includes development controls can be drawn up.[4] Land use can be controlled, with the aim to increase the area covered by open spaces, protect the *agrahāras*, and restrict commercial uses. Viewsheds to the hill can be protected by limiting the height of new construction. Traffic can be regulated by declaring the district as a pedestrian zone with limited vehicular access, especially on festivals. Designated parking areas can be provided at the entry points to the district. Large billboards and other flashy signs can be removed, particularly those in the vicinity of the entry to the temple complex.

Designing for Movement

The above regulatory measures will arrest the decline in the quality of the environment as the urban context of Rockfort is made legible, its traffic controlled, and the imageability of the sacred hill restored to its rightful dominance. To improve the quality of the pilgrim experience however, minor urban design interventions are necessary that would rejuvenate the natural and spatial archetypal forms of the traditional cultural landscape vocabulary. Pilgrimage here is a special kind of journey undertaken for spiritual replenishment that is derived not only from *darshan* (act of beholding) of the temple deities but also from the very physical acts of walking and climbing up the hill. Although the journey does not have to be comfortable, an encounter with nature would do much to sooth the psyche. The pilgrim path, as in yore, should wind through groves with water bodies where the one can interrupt the journey to bathe, rest, and perform ablutions. The orchestrated journey would be a fitting preparation for the goal that is the encounter finally with the gods.

The entries to the cultural heritage district should be marked by tall pillars, framing not only the four streets leading to the Rockfort Temple but also the distant viewsheds to the hill (Fig. 5). An alternative pilgrim path, passing through natural settings and circumventing the commercial, as well as allowing panoramic views of the hill, is proposed for the pilgrim who has to climb a total of 417 rock cut steps to reach the Ucchipillayar temple at the very top (Fig. 6). Along this path would be shady groves of coconut and *pipal* trees, tanks brimming with water with *ghats* (steps) around them, and rest areas in small *mandapams* (Fig. 7). The pilgrim takes this path from the Nandi Kovil Street and begins the journey at the Teppakulam that is redesigned with colonnades running on all four sides of the tank and *ghats* leading down to the water interspersed with small shrines (Fig. 8). From there the stone path takes the pilgrim to the Umayan Kulam at a higher level and Nandavanam with ornamental trees of *jasmine* and *champa*. After bathing and resting here, the pilgrim takes the Rockfort South Street and resumes her climb to the Thayumanavar and Uchippillayar temples with their *mandapas*. The hustle and bustle of urban life feels remotely distant as the pilgrim is transported into the holy environment of devotional chants and worship, and is rewarded with the *darshan* of the deities, panoramic views of the city spread below, and of Kaveri on the horizon.

Conclusion

The integrated conservation approach outlined above can be applied to other temple towns that are bustling centers of religious and commercial activities. They share common patterns of landscape symbolism, have experienced transformation of natural into urban settings over time, and are venues of large-scale pilgrimage tied to temple visits and festivals. As continuing sites of inhabitation they have considerable amount of built heritage of monumental and ordinary buildings. They are significant cultural centers where traditional building skills are still in use, the arts are fostered, and crafts are produced. As such they are custodians of both tangible and intangible heritage. They need help, however, through sensitive planning and management of growth and change. They share common problems of haphazard urban development that threatens their environmental heritage, weak municipal governance, and absence of regulatory framework that will ensure protection. We propose that their core be protected as cultural heritage districts so that both heritage buildings and open areas can be protected, growth can be controlled, and public infrastructure can be improved. Conservation efforts can then be undertaken at the landscape scale improving the quality of those who live there and those who visit.

Notes and References

1 Shiva came to be known as Thayumanavar Swamy meaning one who became the mother, a story that reveals his maternal compassion towards his devotees. When Ratnavati of Tiruchirapalli began suffering from labor pains, her mother could not reach her to help her in her confinement because the river Kaveri was flooding. Shiva appeared as the mother of Ratnavati and delivered her child. When the mother finally reached the daughter, Shiva reappeared in front them as Mattuvarkuzhal Ammai.

This legend is illustrated on the walls and ceiling of Chittra Mandapam within the Rockfort Complex.

2 Other landmarks at the foot of the hill, such as the palace of the Nawab (built by the Nayaks), and that of Clive and Bishop Heber School of the colonial era are part of the built heritage of the city.

3 See *Charter for the Conservation of Unprotected Architectural Heritage and Sites in India,* Unpublished version presented at INTACH Convention, 2004, at http://portal.architexturez.net/site/groups/intach-chtr/041-29. It advocates that urban conservation plans be incorporated into the statutory Master Plans prepared by the Town Planning Departments. This can be done within the Special Area provision of the Town Planning Acts that differ from state to state.

4 This can be done under the revised Tamil Nadu Town and Country Planning Act of 1971. For implementation of the proposed Master Plan, the Town Planning Department should coordinate with the Rockfort Temple Trust, ASI, Tiruchirapalli Development Authority, and the Municipal Corporation.

Fass, V. *The Forts of India*. London: Collins, 1986.

Hudson, D. Kanchipuram in *Temple Towns of Tamil Nadu*, edited by G. Michell, *Marg Publications*, 1993: 18-39.

L'Hernault, F. Tiruvannamalai in *Temple Towns of Tamil Nadu*, edited by G. Michell, *Marg Publications*, 1993: 40-57.

Michell, G. *The Hindu Temple: An Introduction to Its Meaning and Forms*. Chicago: The University of Chicago Press, 1988.

Michell, G. Introduction in *Temple Towns of Tamil Nadu, Marg Publications,* 1993: 2-17.

Michell, G. (ed.) *Eternal Kaveri: Historical Sites Along South Indias Greatest River*, 51, no. 1 (1999).

Moore, L. *Trichinopoly Gazetteer*. New Delhi: Cosmo Publications, 2000.

Nanda, V. Temple City of Kumbakonam in *Eternal Kaveri: Historical Sites Along South India's Greatest River*, edited by G. Michell, 51, no. 1 (1999): 107-122.

Nitz, H., Planned temple towns and Brahmin villages as spatial expressions of the ritual politics of medieval kingdoms in South India in *Ideology and Landscape in Historical Perspective*, edited by G. Beger. New York: Cambridge University Press, 1992:107-124.

Raghunathan, Aparna. *A Design Proposal for the Fort Area of Tiruchirapalli, India*. Unpublished MLA Thesis, University of Illinois at Urbana Champaign, USA, 2003.

Singh, Rana P.B. Life in Historic Urban Landscape of Varanasi, a Heritage City of India in *Proceedings of the International Conference for Integrating Urban Knowledge and Practice*, Gothenburg, Sweden, 2005: 2-18.

Sinha, A. The Conservation of Sacred Sites: Sarnath, A Case Study. *Landscape Research*, 16, no. 3(1991): 23-30.

Sinha, A. Design of Settlements in the Vaastu Shastras. *Journal of Cultural Geography*, 17, no. 2(1998): 27-41.

Sinha, A. Natural Archetypes. *Geographical Review of India*, 62, no. 1 (2000): 26-38.

Sinha, A. Designing Pilgrimage Sites. *Journal of Landscape Architecture*, 1. no. 2 (2001):14-17.

Sinha, A. Sacred Landscapes in India: Forms and Meanings. *Geographical Review of India*, 65, no. 3 (2003): 241-250.

Smith, D. Chidambaram. *Temple Towns of Tamil Nadu*, edited by G. Michell, *Marg Publications*, 1993:58-75.

Description of Plates

1. View of Rockfort temple, Tiruchirapalli
2. View of the entrance *gopuram*, Tiruchirapalli
3. Restricted access to the Teppakulam
4. Proposed Master Plan of the Rockfort Cultural Heritage District
5. Pillars at the entry to the Cultural Heritage District
6. Ucchipillayar Temple on the summit
7. Rest areas on the proposed alternative pilgrim path
8. Redesign of Teppakulam

Aparna and Amita: 1. View of Rockfort temple, Tiruchirapalli

Aparna and Amita: 2. View of the entrance *gopuram*, Tiruchirapalli

Aparna and Amita: 3. Restricted access to the Teppakulam

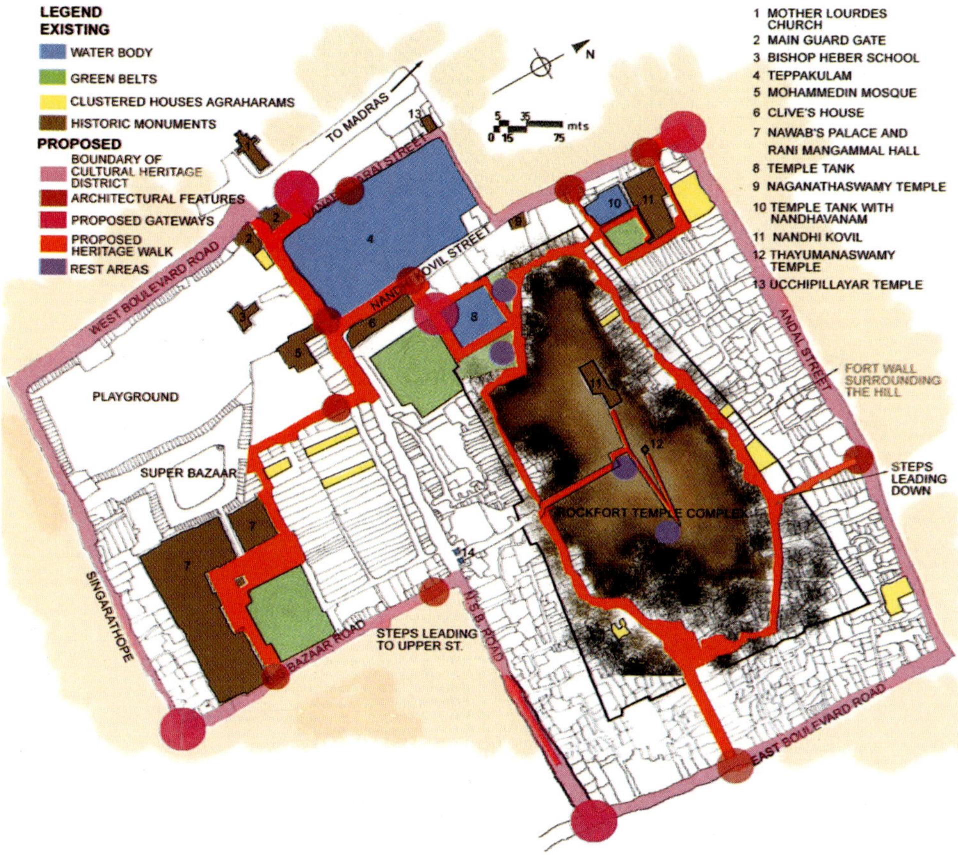

Aparna and Amita: 4. Proposed Master Plan of the Rockfort Cultural Heritage District

Aparna and Amita: 5. Pillars at the entry to the Cultural Heritage District

Aparna and Amita: 6. Ucchipillayar Temple on the summit

Aparna and Amita: 7. Rest areas on the proposed alternative pilgrim path

Aparna and Amita: 8. Redesign of Teppakulam

11

A Sangama of Architectural Styles: The Vidyashankara Temple

Indu Parthasarathy

South Indian scholars have neglected the study of an important Hindu temple, that of Vidyashankara in Shringeri, although in terms of architecture and iconography the temple is an anomaly. This paper is an examination of the structure and style of the temple which reveal artistic modes of confluence of the northern and southern architectural orders and South Indian sculptural styles. The artistic transformation and continuity that we see here throws light on the development of religious concepts and the role of temples and teachers during the Vijayanagara period.

The Vidyashankara temple is unique: it is known by the name of an *āchārya* (scholar and teacher) who formulated religious and philosophical doctrine than by the icon enshrined in the sanctum. In fact, Shringeri is named after sage Rishyashringa who is mentioned in the *Ramayana*.[1] A greater and more well known *āchārya* or *guru* associated with Shringeri is Adi Shankaracharya who established a pontificate there during the ninth century. The famous *āchārya* reintegrated the various sects of Hinduism under a common banner, called *shanmatha-sthāpanāchārya* as he brought together six gods or rather ways of worship, namely Vishnu, Shiva, Devi, Surya, Ganapati and Kumara. The sage recognized that the survival of *sanātanadharma* depended both on the revival of

Vedanta philosophy as well as the reorganization of the monastic life of India. With this objective, Shankaracharya founded *mathas* and *pīthas* all over the country. The pontificate established at Shringeri is known as the Shri Sharada Pitha where an image of Sharada is above an image of Sri Chakra *yantra*.

The Vidyashankara temple was built to commemorate sage Vidyathirtha (also called Vidyashankara), the tenth pontiff of the *matha* and is considered to be his *sanjeevani samadhi* as it is believed that the sage disappeared at that spot while performing *lambik yoga*. He was the preceptor of Vidyaranya, the twelfth *guru* of the lineage, who had inspired the brothers Harihara and Bukka to establish the *karnataka simhasana* in order to rejuvenate Hinduism by the establishment of the Vijayanagara empire. The temple was, in fact, constructed under the supervision of the pontiffs Bharathi Tirtha and Vidyaranya. The Vidyashankara shrine existed in some form during this period which we can gather from two inscriptions dated c.1346 C.E. and c.1356 C.E.,which pertain to the visits of Harihara and Bukka to Shringeri and their gifts of land to Bharati Tirtha.[2]

The Vidyashankara temple at Shringeri is in the Chickamagalur district of Karnataka, on the River Tungabhadra. Built of reddish brown granite, the temple is a striking example of the fusion of different architectural influences and traditions. However, this had been a dominant feature in the art of Karnataka from ancient times. As Karnataka was strategically placed between the northern and southern cultural traditions, the practices of the adjoining regions inevitably percolated into the ethos of the people. The stylistic transmutation of styles in Karnataka became visible in the art of the Satavahanas (second century B.C.E to second century C.E.). They brought the Buddhist artistic traditions of Sanchi and Bharhut to the Deccan, to the rock excavations at Maharashtra (Bedsa, Karla, Ajanta) and Andhra Pradesh (Amaravati, Nagarajunakonda). The prototypes of later architectural forms can be discerned in Amaravati, in the use of molded *kapotas* or cornices, *shālas* or wagon shaped roof-tops, the square and circular *kutas or* (roofs terminating at a point), and apsidal and many storied structures. The *kuta, shāla* and *panjara* (apsidal) forms became essential decorative motifs in the southern *vimanas* where they were seen on the *tālas or* storeys of the superstructure.[3] The *chaitya* window (shaped like a horse shoe), which was common in Buddhist architecture was incorporated in Hindu temple architecture as a design motif.

With the decline of the Satavahanas in the Deccan, the cultural center and focus of political power shifted to Kanchipuram under the Pallavas. However, in the fourth century the Kadamba dynasty made its appearance under Mayurasharma from their capital in Banavasi in northern Karnataka.[4] Though not known as prolific builders they contributed to the development of an idiom in respect to the *shikhara*, which came to be known as the Kadamba Nagara style. It is characterized by a series of horizontal layers, which tapered into a pyramid with the tooth like ornamentation (dentil) on every tier.[5]

During the sixth century, the Chalukyas of Badami emerged as a powerful dynasty and were powerful contenders for the hegemony of *dakshināpathi*. It was inevitable that they were in constant conflict with their neighboring kingdoms to preserve this position. A positive result of this interaction (albeit hostile) was that the Chalukyan rule encouraged a period of intense creative activity resulting in a treasure trove of temples being built in northern Karnataka (Badami, Aihole, Pattadakal and Mahakuta). One can see here an assemblage of temples representing the Dravida, Vesara, Nagara and other hybrid orders of architecture. The Chalukyas ruled over parts of Maharashtra and Gujarat, Kalinga and south Kosala till Kanchipuram and parts of Kerala. Such diverse cultural contacts led to a synthesis of styles. Some of the early Gupta influences are reflected in its art, such as the finely carved doorways, *jālandaras* or window screens, sculpted wall panels and in the personified river goddesses Ganga and Yamuna. The most significant aspect of confluence was in the variety of *shikharas* in the temples: the Rekha Nagara curvilinear spire on the Papanatha and Jambulinga temples at Pattadakal; the Kadamba Nagara variant may be exemplified by the Mallikarjuna temple at Aihole, while the southern *vimāna* form with its octagonal Dravida, square Nagara and apsidal or circular Vesara *shikhara* as seen in the Virupaksha temple at Pattadakal.[6]

It was with the Pallavas of Kanchi, that the Chalukyas had their maximum artistic exchange resulting in a transmutation of styles. It is known through inscriptional evidences that Vikramaditya II, after his victory over the Pallavas, built the Virupaksha temple by employing Pallava sculptors from Kanchipuram. The Pallavas in turn may have been inspired by the bold and vigorous sculptural style of the Chalukyas. The Pallava rendering of Simha Vishnu with his two wives and the Ananthashayin image at Mahabalipuram closely follow the Chalukyan depiction of Harihara and two consorts and the Vishnu reliefs at Badami. Thus the impact of Chalukyas was far reaching as can be seen in the rock cut Kailasanatha temple at Ellora dated to the ninth century built under the aegis of the next major dynasty to rule in the Deccan, namely the Rashtrakutas. The Kailasanatha temple is similar to the Virupaksha at Pattadakal, which was in turn similar to the Pallava Dharmaraja *ratha* at Mahabalipuram.

The Gangas of Talakad rose to prominence in the southern and western parts of Karnataka around the fourth century and lingered on till the eleventh century with wavering political fortunes. Their unique contribution to Karnataka architecture is their sustained preference to the distinctive southern idiom for their temples. The Chalukyas re-emerged in the tenth century from their capital at Kalyan. They were prolific builders and set the stage for the Kakatiya and Hoysala efflorescence in architecture. The skill of the Kalyani Chalukyan artist is evident in the Holal Inscription, dated c.1231 C.E., found at the Amriteshvara temple. It mentions a *sutradhari* who was a Vishvakarman of the Kali age, a master of the sixty four arts, an expert in building the sixty four types of *prāsāda,* the one who had built the *chaturjati*-the Nagara, Kalinga, Dravida and

Vesara.[7] The Kalyani Chalukyas selected soft chlorite schist as their building medium and this dictated many innovations in construction. Since soft stone could not carry any heavy superstructures, the tower became reduced in height. To counteract this reduction in height and to create a balanced appearance, a plinth was provided which had many masonry courses. The molded raised *pītha* was seen elsewhere too, as in the eleventh century Solanki temples at Gujarat. The gradual expansion of the temple walls into *rathas* was seen on the medieval temples at Central India (Khajuraho) and Orissa and there may have been a mutual exchange of designs between the regions. The *bahyabhitti* or outer walls of the Kalyani Chalukyan temples were embellished with architectural and geometric motifs like pilasters, *pūrnakumbhas* and scrollwork.[8]

The Hoysalas, who gained importance in the early years of the eleventh century, developed the Kalyani Chalukyan features in architecture and created their own unique style. They continued the use of chlorite schist, which gave them great scope for embellishment in carving. The typical Hoysala temple stands on a high plinth, which allowed an open *pradakshinapatha*. A distinctive feature of this style is that regardless of the multiplicity of the component elements, the structure always appears as an organic whole. The usual parts of a Hoysala temple are the *garbhagriha* or sanctum, the *antarala* or vestibule, the *navaranga* or hall with nine bays, and these are fused into a unit.[9] The raised plinth, which provides an open space around the temple and the continuous bands of friezes that encircle the structure contribute to the compact appearance. The continuation of the stellate and multiangled plan of the *garbhagrihas* and *maṇḍapas* into the walls and *shikhara* further emphasize the unitary nature of the Hoysala temple. The Hoysala *shikhara* is a blend of the southern and northern spires. The northern spires appear as a cohesive unit and suggest an upwardly soaring movement. The southern spires on the other hand emphasize horizontality and assume a paramedical shape created by receding tiers of *tālas*. The capping device on the northern *shikhara* is a flattened and ribbed *amalaka*, while the crowning element in the southern style is a polygonal cupola. The Hoysala *shikhara* accepts the unitary character and the *sukhanasika* (portion projecting from the *shikhara* and roofing the *antarala*), of the northern idiom, but is generally capped with a *kalasha* finial. The movement or rhythm of the Hoysala superstructure is neither strongly vertical nor horizontal, but somewhere in-between. The articulation on the walls of this period is distinctive and has three discernable sections- the base with friezes, the middle part with images under lush canopies and arches and the upper part with miniature shrine motifs. The many offsets and projections of the base create the renowned Hoysala stellate plan.

The Vijayanagara dynasty came into existence in the fourteenth century and continued up to the seventeenth century. Zealously guarding their role as protectors of the faith, the Vijayanagara kings encouraged the renovation and enlargement of the existing temples all over the south of India. They built several *prākāras* or enclosure walls, with imposing *gopuras* or gateways around the temple complex and there was an increase in the number of subsidiary shrines and *maṇḍapas*. The massive, monolithic, composite pillars of diverse designs are the hallmark of this style, which was really an elaboration of the Pandya idiom. The Vijayanagara architects adopted the use of granite as the building material. The temples built in their northern domains of Karnataka and Andhra Pradhesh, retained much of the Chalukya-Hoysala-Kakatiya inspiration while further south they retained Pallava-Chola-Pandya traditions.[10] To exemplify, a few early temples built in the erstwhile Hoysala country, such as the Male Mallikarjuna temple at Arsikere, have high plinths.[11] However, the mature Vijayanagara style is similar to the southern style, but the wall treatment in Vijayanagara temples soon moved away from Hoysala influences. Alternating projections and recesses marked by full-length pilasters relieved the surfaces. The projected areas had deep niches, while the recesses depicted single pillars emerging from *kalashas* (*kumbhapanjaras*).[12] Similar decorative pillars had been carved in the Badami Chalukya period and had been used often by Chola artists as a decorative motif.[13] Thus, although the Vidyashankara temple, technically belongs to the Vijayanagara style, at first glance it appears Hoysala in style, mainly due to the raised plinth, the stellate plan, the sculptural style, the circular shape of the *shikhara* and the presence of the *navaranga* and *sukhanasika*.

The Vidyashankara temple consists of a *garbhagriha* which houses a *linga* called Vidyashankara. It faces east and forms the nucleus of a *panchayatana* complex. There are three shrines: to the south, west and north of the sanctum. A four-headed image of Brahma with Saraswati occupies the south cella, a *chaturbhuja* Narayana with Lakshmi idol is in the western shrine and an Uma Maheshwara icon is housed in the north shrine. Two more shrines are found in front of the *garbhagriha* on either side of the *antarala* which contain a Vidya Ganapati and a Mahishasuramardini, Durga. The positioning of a group of deities around the sanctum is in keeping with the inclusive philosophy of Adi Shankara, the founder of the Shringeri pontificate.

The elliptical plan of the temple is its outstanding feature. From the base to the *āditāla* (first storey of the temple) and *maṇḍapaprastara* (entablature) it is a *chapa* or double apse.[14] The western apse contains the *garbhagriha* and *antarala*, which faces the main entrance on the east. The Navaranga on the east, and apsidal in form is an abrupt departure from the popular stellar and cruciform plans favored by the Hoysala builders of that region. Though uncommon, the apsidal plan has a hoary past and has a close association with Buddhist architecture. The Chikka Mahadeva at Mahakuta is an early example of an apsidal temple in Karnataka. An important, early eighth century apsidal (*gajaprishta* form) temple is the Durga temple at Aihole, belonging to the early phase in Chalukyan architecture. The temple has a raised apsidal *upapītha* on which the apsidal shrine stands. A closed *pradakshina* stands on the *upapītha* which has a row of peripheral pillars ranged round the structure. The *adishthana* expands into eleven bays. The Vidyashankara temple bears a similarity to the Durga temple, though approximately seven hundred years separate the two structures. Both are *sandhara* (having a covered inner *pradakshinapatha* around the sanctum), apsidal shrines standing on raised *pītha*. The Durga temple has a Nagara *shikhara* (in a damaged condition, and probably of a later date), while the Vidyashankara temple has a variation of the same for its superstructure, although the flat roofing over the *maṇḍapas* in both the temples are of the same type.

A special significance is attributed to the choice of an apsidal plan for the Vidyashankara temple. The form has been arrived at by the mingling of a square (*bhadra*) type plan with a circular (*vritta*) one. The circle resembles a Sri Chakra (the geometric *yantra* composed of overlapping triangles symbolizing the goddess). It may be possible that in this temple, the circular plan denoting the Sri Chakra had been divided into two halves (the two apses), enclosing the square as Adi Shankaracharya had installed the *yantra* at Shringeri. The use of an apsidal plan after a long interval seems justified when one considers his association with the Sri Chakra. The front part of the Vidyashankara temple is also apsidal, and a definite departure from the norm. The two apses if placed next to each other can form a sixteen-pointed stellate plan, which had been popular with the Hoysala builders for the *garbhagriha*. The use of Sri Chakra with its sixteen–petalled lotus was an integral part of the *yantra* and of the architectural plan of the temple.

Other departures might be seen in the height of the *adishthana* which has been increased by the addition of the *upapītha*, and reveals the *upana*, *jagati, kapota* and *pattika*. The last unit is commonly seen on southern *adishthanas*. Six projected tiers with five recessed sculpted intervals form the *adishthana* of the temple. A pleasing textural effect is created by the rows of drops carved on the lower surface of the tiers. A marked Hoysala influence is seen in the treatment of the *adishthana*, both stylistically (multiple tiers, provision for the *pradakshinapatha* and the angled plan) and thematically (rows of elephants, lions, riders, *hamsa*s and narrative panels). The *bahybhitti* is divided by a series of pilasters enclosing niches of the *torana* type containing within. Each pilaster has a tall fluted shaft with a square base. A *malasthana* is found at the top, and the abacus consists of a *kalasha*, saucer shaped *tadi*, a bulbous *kumuda* topped by an inverted *padma* molding and a *phalaka* upon which the beams of the entablature rest. The use of pilasters to divide space was a device seen in the mature Vijayanagara style, where the projections and recessions of the wall surfaces were marked by engaged columns. The convex parts of the two apses are thrown into seven major *bhadras* (projections from the walls), resembling the *saptaratha* mode of the Orissan temples. The double flexure of the eaves shows a continuation of the Chalukyan mode. The *prastara* reveals a Vijayanagara innovation in that its underside is sculpted with curved ribs and crossbars while the monolithic stone chain links hanging from the *kapotas* which became a common feature in Vijayanagara temples.

The Vidyashankara temple has six doorways, each with a set of seven steps leading to the door while elephants and *vyālas*, a Vijayanagara feature, flank these stairs. There is a corresponding *sopana* (stairway) of six steps leading up the *upapitha*. The miniature shrines flanking the entrances seen on Hoysala temples are absent here. The doorways are guarded by *dvarapalas,* two each of Shaiva, Vaishnava and Shakta affiliation, and show an obvious Hoysala mode of ornamentation. Each door has an ornate doorframe with *sākha* components and a projecting door cornice, which suggests a Chalukya- Kakatiya influence. The river goddesses Ganga and Yamuna are represented on their *vāhanas* in their usual place at the base of the doorjambs and a Gajalakshmi adorns the lintel-motifs which persist from the Gupta period.

The *navaranga manḍapa* occupies the eastern apse of the temple. Twelve peripheral monolithic pillars range around the square *manḍapa*. Though the four central pillars have been eliminated in the design, the *navaranga* concept is suggested by the nine, coffered bays on the ceiling. The central bay is the largest and has great depth with the beautiful design of a lotus. The pillars are referred to as the Rasi pillars as each one is dedicated to a sign of the zodiac. Architecture is planned in such a way that at sunrise, the first rays of the sun falls on the pillars which depict the *rasi* through which the sun is traversing. On the floor is inscribed a large circle divided by many convergent lines, indicating the shadows cast by the pillars when the sun's rays fall on them. On one face of the lowermost square on each of the twelve pillars is a sign of the zodiac; such as the bull representing the Vrishabha *rasi*. The next section of the pillar depicts the presiding deity of the sign. For instance, Sukra is the *pradhana devata* of the Vrishabha constellation and is therefore represented on the same pillar. When one enters the *manḍapa* through the eastern entrance, the Mesha *rasi* pillar is on the right. Moving in the *pradakshina* order, the following pillar depicts the Vrishabha *rasi* and so on, till one completes the *manḍapa* with the twelfth pillar, that of the Meena *rasi*. The depiction of the zodiac signs in the *navaranga* in this manner is unique to the Vidyashankara temple. The Rasi *manḍapa* is the forerunner of the grand and ornate halls for which the Vijayanagara dynasty was known. The pillars are of the composite type with rearing *vyālas,* crouching elephants, columnettes and corbelled brackets. The typical Pandya *pushpa potikas* and movable stone balls in the mouth of the *vyālas* are part of the exuberant Vijayanagara style. The high level of ornamentation seen on the pillars and the difference in rendering between the interior and exterior carvings suggest a later date for the *manḍapa* or at least different craftsmen.

The *shikhara* of the temple consists of three sets of tiers rising as a tapering pyramid. It is a *chatushtalavimāna, sandhara, with* three *tālas* raised over the sanctum. A large *sukhanasika* emerges from the *shikhara*, covering the *antarala* below. It has a barrel shaped roof with the *mukhapatti* of the *torana* type. The long channel and hood stones radiating from the second *tāla* create a sloping roof which is a necessity in that region, which receives heavy rainfall. A series of seven, five and three *kapotas* form the second, third and fourth *tālas* of the superstructure. The tooth shaped dentil decoration on the *kapotas* echo the *shikhara* of the Lakshmidevi temple at Doddagaddavalli, an early Hoysala temple. Similar *shikharas,* which are akin to the Phamsana type of superstructures, have been found elsewhere in the Vijayanagara period, as in the cluster of shrines atop the Hemakuta hill, near Hampi.

The Vidyashankara spire differs from the Doddagaddavalli *shikhara* due to the separation of the tiers by *tālas*. The pronounced *tālas* emphasize horizontality like the southern *shikharas*, but the *kuta-shāla- panjara* scheme of the southern *hara* is absent here. Vertical offsets or *bhadras* flanked by engaged pillars are seen on the *tāla harmya* which is a southern feature. The Nagara overtones of the Vidyashankara *shikhara* is evident from the presence of the *sukhanasika* and the curvilinear shape suggests a *rekha* affiliation. However the curve or rhythm of the spire differs from the northern counterpart. It is neither like the Hoysala spire, which appears smaller and more compact and does not have a prominent *tāla* system. The *griva* and the globular *shikhara* show offsets corresponding with the ribbed *tālas* below. The southern influence is suggested by the four Nandis perched on the last *tāla,* as the *lanchanas* of the deity. The four *mahanasika*s on the globular and ribbed *shikhara* face the four directions, which is a Chola feature. The *nasikas* are topped with metal finials. The four cardinal metal *kalashas* and the central one on the *stupi* together forms a *panchakalasha* scheme, which is described in Buddhist texts as a requirement for a *divya vimana*.[15]

The exterior of the Vidyashankara temple is richly carved with numerous sculptures, which when viewed thematically follow the philosophy of Shankara, who had espoused an eclectic approach to Hinduism. The cults of Brahma, Vishnu and Shiva have been well represented by the Nava Brahma group as well as the Dashavatara and the many *samhara* and *kalyana* forms of Shiva. A charming depiction of Gayatri seated within a circular *prabhavali,* on a *ratha* (chariot) type of shrine occupies a prominent position. Sculptures such as that of Chandra, a six headed Kartikkeya, a pleasing Nrittya Ganapathi and an imposing Rajarajeshvari panel are some of the icons, which draw the eye of the beholder. The depictions of Yama and Mrityu are interesting from an iconographic point of view. An image of a standing Shankaracharya, holding a *pustaka* and showing the *varada mudra* occupies a niche.

The narrative panels depict incidents from the epics and stories from Adi Shankaracharya's life. The *āchārya* has been shown teaching four disciples. Eleven other *āchāryas* have also been shown alongside and refer perhaps to the *guruparampara*, commencing with the first appointed pontiff Sureshwaracharya, to Vidyaranya, the preceptor to the first Vijayanagara kings. An *ashvamedha* sacrifice and a royal wedding have also been delineated. Some interesting yogic postures have been demonstrated in the carvings. Interspersed across the sculpted bands are mythical, hybrid animals and *ganas* (dwarfish persons generally shown playing music or dancing), which is typical of the Vijayanagara repertoire. There is a drastic loss of detail and embellishment and the friezes are neither dense nor as lively as the Hoysala carvings.

Although the sculptures appear to be of the Hoysala idiom, a closer look reveals that they do not display the heavy ornamentation of the preceding period. There are no foliated canopies, neither *madanikas*, nor the elaborate miniature shrines enclosing the figures of deities. The style is more austere, simple and contained and appear to be the work of artists used to the soft stone technique, working in unfamiliar hard stone. However as far as the costume and jewelry are concerned, the Hoysala influence is obvious. The depiction of heavy and profuse jewelry on the images was a typical Hoysala feature and this can be seen in the garland *vyjayanti*. It emerges from the back of the image on the right side, loops across the knees and moves up to the necklace on the left side of the image. The depiction of drapery, especially the jeweled skirt, *urubandha* was not given importance by the Hoysalas, but here, the folds of the costume are clearly incised. The weapons and other attributes held by the gods and goddesses are no longer swamped by tassels as on Hoysala sculptures and are closer in style to the southern idiom. The torsos of the images have been delineated in a naturalistic manner, with a hint at musculature, unlike the heavy and ponderous depictions of the preceding period. The Vidyashankara sculptures represent a transitional phase. The work is neither rigid and formalized enough to be recognized as

Vijayanagara, nor are they as decorative as Hoysala. Vestiges of a Chola style can be traced in this temple–slender and graceful figures were often depicted with a slight *bhanga*. Garments cling to the body and a moderate amount of jewelry adorns it. This quality of simple ornamentation and compactness is evident in Chola work, and is occasionally found in the sculptures of the Vidyashankara temple.

The Vidyashankara *shikhara* defies categorization. It may at best be described as a variation of the Kadamba Nagara style: a low superstructure that is a stepped pyramid of receding tiers separated from one another by recessed necks. The temple is an amalgamation of diverse artistic traditions of India which have been harmoniously blended–a *sangama* of art forms and religious concepts.

Notes and References

1 According to the Ramayana, Rishyashringa presided over the *putrakameshti* rite performed by Dasaratha.

2 A.K.Shastry, *A History of Sringeri* (Dharwad: 1982), 17ff.

3 K.R. Srinivasan, Andhras and Ikshavakus and Litrary Sources in *Encyclopedia of Indian Temple Architecture,* ed. Michael W. Meister and M.A. Dhaky (New Delhi: 1983), 14.

4 Phalaksha, *History of Karnataka* (Tiptur: 1989), 40.

5 R.N.Saletore, *Vijayanagara Art,* (New Delhi: 1982), 45.

6 K.V.Soundara Rajan, *Early Temple Architecture in Karnataka and its Ramifications* (Dharwad: 1969), 40.

7 M.K. Dhaky, *Indian Temple Forms in Karnata Inscriptions and Architecture* (New Delhi: 1977), 3.

8 B.K. Gururaja Rao, Chalukya Influences on Hoysala Architecture, in *Chalukyas of Kalyan* ed. M.S. Nagaraja Rao, (Bangalore: 1983), 179.

9 Foekema Gerard, *A Complete Guide to the Hoysala Temples* (New Delhi: 1996).

10 K.R.Srinivasan, *Temples of South India* (New Delhi: 1967), 167.

[11] S.N.Shivarudraswamy, *Vijayanagara Temples in Karnataka* (Mysore: 1996), 71.

[12] George Michell, *Architecture and Art of South India* (Cambridge: 1995), 28.

[13] Shivarudraswamy, op. cit., 82.

[14] Srinivasan, op. cit., 173.

[15] Ibid., 179.

Description of Plates

1. General view, Vidyashankara temple, Shringeri
2. Vidyashankara temple, Shringeri
3. Doorway, Vidyashankara temple
4. Vidyashankara temple
5. Vidyashankara temple
6. Vidyashankara temple
7. Gayatri, Vidyashankara temple, Shringeri
8. Stone chains, Vidyashankara temple, Shringeri
9. Interior Pillar, Vidyashankara temple, Shringeri
10. Plan, Vidyashankara temple, Shringeri

Indu Parthsarathy: 1. General view, Vidyashankara temple, Shringeri

Indu Parthsarathy: 2. Vidyashankara temple, Shringeri

Indu Parthsarathy: 3. Doorway, Vidyashankara temple

Indu Parthsarathy: 4. Vidyashankara temple

Indu Parthsarathy: 5. Vidyashankara temple

Indu Parthsarathy: 6. Vidyashankara temple

Indu Parthsarathy: 7. Gayatri, Vidyashankara temple, Shringeri

Indu Parthsarathy: 8. Stone chains, Vidyashankara temple, Shringeri

Indu Parthsarathy: 9. Interior Pillar, Vidyashankara temple, Shringeri

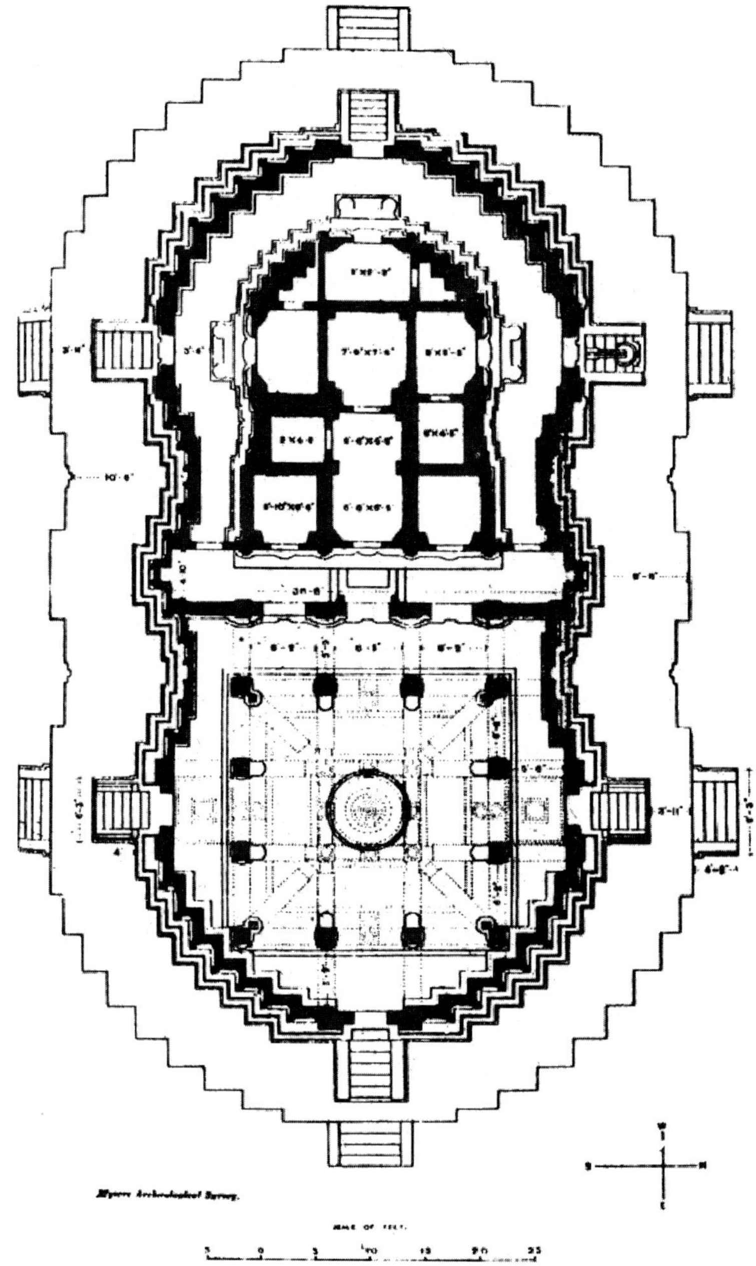

Indu Parthsarathy: 10. Plan, Vidyashankara temple, Shringeri

Select Bibliography

Nalini Rao

Primary Sources

Epigraphical and Archaeological Sources

Annual Reports of Archaeological Survey of India, Calcutta/Delhi, Archaeological Survey of India, 1903-24.

Annual Reports of the Mysore Archaeological Department, Bangalore/Mysore, Govt. Press, 1910-17, 1922-58.

Annual Reports on South Indian Epigraphy, Madras/Calcutta, Govt. Press, 1889, 1935-39.

Annual Reports on Indian Epigraphy, New Delhi, Manager of Publications, 1947 onwards.

Epigraphia Carnatica, Edited by Lewis Rice and others, Vols. 1, 4, 23, Madras/ Bangalore/Mysore, 1886-1958.

Epigraphia Indica, Vols. 1 (1892), 4 (1896-97), 23 (1925-26).

The Historical Inscriptions of Southern India (Collected till 1923) and Outlines of Political History, By Robert Sewell, Edited by S.K.Aiyangar, Madras, University of Madras, 1932, Reprint, New Delhi, Asian Educational Services, 1983.

Lists of Inscriptions and Sketch of the Dynasties of Southern India, By Robert Sewell, 2 Vols., Madras, Superintendent,Government Press,1884.

South Indian Inscriptions, Vols.1, 4, 9, 17, 20, New Series, Vol. 16.

Vijayanagara Inscriptions, Edited by B. R. Gopal, 2 Vols., Mysore, Directorate of Archaeology and Museums, 1985-1986.

Contemporary Literary Works

Amuktamalyada of Krishnadeva Raya, Edited by Venkataraya Shastry, Lingasetividhi, Madras, University of Madras, 1963.

Sources of Vijayanagar History, Edited by S. Krishnaswami Aiyangar, Madras, University of Madras, 1919, Reprint, Delhi, Gian Publishing House, 1986.

Accounts of Foreign Visitors

Sewell, Robert, *A Forgotten Empire (Vijayanagar): A Contribution to the History of India*, London, Swan Sonnenschein & Co., 1900, Reprint, New Delhi, Asian Educational Services, 1983.

Secondary Sources

Aiyangar, S.K., "Foundation of Vijayanagar," *Quarterly Journal of the Mythic Society* 2, No.1 (1920), 13-32.

Appadurai, Arjun, "Worship and Conflict in South India" Unpublished Ph.D. dissertation, University of Chicago, 1976.

Breckenridge, Carol, "The Sri Minaksi Sundaresvarar Temple: Worship and Endowments in South India, 1833-1925." Unpublished Ph.D dissertation University of Wisconsin, Madison, 1976.

Dallapiccola, Anna Libera and Lallemant, Stephanie Zingel-Ave, Editors, *Vijayanagara – City and Empire*: New Currents of Research, 2 Vols. Stuttgart: Franz Steiner Verlag Wiesbaden, GMBH, 1985.

Dallapiccola, A.L. and Verghese, Anila, *Sculpture at Vijayanagara Iconography and Style*, New Delhi, Manohar Publications and the American Institute of Indian Studies, 1998.

Davidson, Job Thomas, "Cultural Developments in Tamil Nadu during the Vijayanagara Period." In *Vijayanagara – City and Empire*, pp. 5-40. Edited by A. L. Dallapiccola and S. Z. Lallemant, Vol. 1. Stuttgart: Franz Steiner Verlag Wiesbaden, GMBH, 1985.

Davison-Jenkins, D.J., *The Irrigation and Water Supply Systems of the city of Vijayanagara,* New Delhi, Manohar Publications and the American Institute of Indian Studies, New Delhi, 1997.

Desayi, Pandurangarav Bhimarava, *Vijayanagar Samrajya*, Dharwad, Vijayanagara Smarakotsva Mandala, 1936.

Devaraj, D.V and Patil, C.S., Editors, *Vijayanagara: Progress of Research 1987-1988*, Directorate of Archaeology and Museums, Mysore, 1991.

Dikshit, G.S., Editor, *Early Vijayanagara*. Studies in its History and Culture (Proceedings of S. Srikantaya Centenary Seminar), Bangalore, 1988.

"S. Srikantaya on Vidyaranya's Part in the Foundation of Vijayanagara" *In Early Vijayanagara*, pp. 39-45, Edited by G.S.Dikshit, Bangalore, B.M.S. Memorial Foundation, 1988.

Filliozat, Vasundhara, *L' Epigraphie de Vijayanagar du debut a 1377*, Paris: Ecole Francaise d' Extreme Orient, 1973.

Filliozat,V., "Hampi—Vijayanagara" *In Early Vijayanagara*, Edited by G. S. Dikshit, Bangalore, B.M.S. Foundation,1988, 179-190.

Filliozat,V., *Hampi-Vijayanagara: The Temple of Vitthala*, New Delhi, Sitaram Bharatiya Institute of Scientific Research, 1991.

Fritz, J. M.George Michell; and M.S.Nagaraja Rao, *Where Kings and Gods Meet*, the Royal Centre at Vijayanagara, *India*, Tucson, Arizona, University of Arizona Press, 1984.

Fritz, J. M., "Vijayanagara: Auhority and Meaning of a South Indian Imperial Capital" *American anthropologist,* 88 (1) 1986, 44-55.

Jackson, William, *Vijayanagaa Voices*, Hampshire, Ashgate, 2005.

Kamat, Jyotsna K, *Social Life in Medieval Karnataka*. New Delhi, Abhinav Publications, 1980, Oxford University Press, 1984.

Katti, Madhav, N., Some Important Epigraphs of the Sangama Dynasty in *Early Vijayanagara*, pp. 143-152. Edited by G. S. Dikshit, Bangalore, B.M.S. Memorial Foundation,1988.

Longhurst, A. H., *Hampi Ruins: Described and Illustrated*, Madras, Government Press, 1917, Reprint, New Delhi, Asian Educational Services, (1988).

Michell, George, *Vijayanagara: Architectural Inventory of the Urban Core,* 2 Vols., Directorate of archaeology and Museums, Mysore, 1990.

Michell, G., *The Vijayanagara Courtly Style: Incorporation and Syntheseis in the Royal Architecture of Southern India, 15th-17th Centuries,* New Delhi, Manohar Publications and the American Institute of Indian Studies, 1992.

Michell, G., *The New Cambridge History of India* 1.6: Architecture and Art of Southern India-Vijayanagara and the Successor States, Cambridge University Press, Cambridge, 1995.

Michell, G. and Filliozat V., Editors, *Splendours of the Vijayanagara Empire, Hampi*, Bombay, Marg Publications, 1981.

Nagaraja Rao, M. S., Editor, *Vijayanagara: Progress of Research 1979-1983*, Mysore, Directorate of Archaeology and Museums, 1983.

Nagaraja Rao, and Patil, C. S., "Epigraphical References to City Gates and Watch Towers of Vijayanagara" In *Vijayanagara: Progress of Research 1983-1984,* Edited by M.S. Nagaraja Rao, Mysore, Directorate of Archaeology and Museums, 1985, 96-99.

Nagaraja Rao, M. S. (ed.), *Vijayanagara: Through the Eyes of* Alexander J Greenlaw, 1856 (and) John Gollings, 1983, *Myso*re, Directorate of Archaeology and Museums, 1988.

Narasimhaiah, B., "A Decade of Excavation at Vijayanagara (Hampi)" In *Early Vijayanagara*, Edited by G.S. Dikshit, Bangalore, B.M.S. Memorial Foundation, 1988, 191-222.

Narasimhaiah B., *Metropolis of Vijayanagara: Significance of Remains of Citadel*, Delhi, Book India Publishing Co., 1992.

Rajasekhara, Sindigi, *Masterpieces of Vijayayanagara Art,* Bombay, Taraporevala, 1983.

Rama Sharma, M. H., *The History of the Vijayanagar Empire*, Edited by M. H. Gopal, Bombay, Popular Prakashan,1978-80, Vol. 1. *Beginnings and Expansion 1308-1569*, 1978, Vol. 2. *Decline and Disappearance,* 1980.

Rao, Gurti Venket Rao, "Krishna Deva Raya and the Portuguese" *Journal of the Andhra Historical Research Society* 10, Parts 1- 4 (1936-37), 73-85.

Rao, Nalini, 'Royal Portraits at Vijayangara:Identification and Meaning, In *New Trends in Indian Art and Archaeology: S.R. Rao's 70th Birthday Felicitation* Volume, vol. 2, Edited by B.U. Nayak and N.C.Ghosh, New Delhi, Aditya Prakashan,1992, 349-366.

Rao, Nalini, "The Heroic Tradition in South Indian Art: Ascetics, Gods, and Kings" In *Ananya: A Portrait of India*, Edited by S.N.Sridhar and Nirmal K.Mattoo, NY, The Association of Indians in America,1997, 523-543.

Rao, Nalini, *Royal Artistic Imagery at Vijayanagara* (New Delhi, Munshiram Manoharlal) (Forthcoming).

Ratnam, Venkata A.V., *Local Government in the Vijayanagara Empire,* Mysore, University of Mysore, 1972.

Ravenshaw, E.C., "Translations of Various Inscriptions Found Among the Ruins of Vijayangara,with Preliminary Observation by H. H. Wilson." *Asiatic Researches* 20, (1836), 1-40.

Saletore, B.A., *Social and Political Life in the Vijayanagara Empire A.D. 1346-1646*, 2 Vols., Madras, B.G. Paul & Co., 1934, *Vijayangara Art*, New Delhi, Sundeep Prakashan, 1982.

Saraswati, Rangaswami A., "Political Maxims of the Emperor-Poet, Krishnadeva Raya" Translated, *Journal of Indian History* 4, (1925), 61-88.

Sastri, Nilakanta K.A., *A History of South India from Prehistoric Times to the Fall of Vijayanagar*, London, Oxford University Press, 1955.

Sastri, Nilakanta K.A., and Venkataramanayya, N. *Further Sources of Vijayanagara History,* 3 Vols., Madras, Madras University Press, 1946.

Spink, W., "Vijayanagara—City of Victory" *Journal of Indian History 51,* No. I (1973), 123-140.

Srimamamurthy, Y., "Political History of Udayagirirajya during the Vijayanagara Period A.D. 1328-1514" *Journal of Indian History* 12, Nos. 121-123, Parts 1-3, (1963), 526-541.

Srinivasachar, S., text and Satyan, T.S., Photographs, *Hampi:The Fabled Capital of the Vijayanagara Empire,* Mysore, Directorate of Archaeology and Museums, 1995.

Suranarain Row, B., *A Short Description of the City of Vijayanagara,* Madras, Addison & Co., 1909.

Swaminathan,K.D., *Nayakas of Ikkeri,* Madras, P. Varadachary & Co., 57.

Talbot, Cynthia, "Temples, Donors and Gifts:Patterns of Patronage in Thirteenth Century South India" *Journal of Asian Studies*, 50, 2 (May 1991), 308-340.

Venkataramanayya, N., *Studies in the History of the Third Dynasty of Vijayanagara*, Madras, University of Madras, 1936.

Venkataramanayya, N., "Vijayanagara" In *The History and Culture of the Indian People,* Vol. 6, *The Delhi Sultanate,* pp. 762-835, Delhi, Bharatiya Vidya Bhavan, 1960, 762-835.

Verghese, Anila, *Religious Traditions at Vijayanagara: As Revealed Through its Monuments,* New Delhi, Manohar Publications and the American Institute of Indian Studies, New Delhi, 1995.

Verghese,Anila, *Hampi: Monumental Legacy*, Oxford University Press, 2002.

Wagoner, P. B., *Tidings of the King: An Account of Krshnadevaraya of Vijayanagara,* translated from the Telugu *Rayavacakamu,* with and Introduction, Honolulu, University of Hawaii Press, 1993.

Contributors

Vatsa Kumar

Dr. Robert Brown has a Ph.D in Indian Art History from University of California at Los Angeles. He is a Professor of Art History, University of California at Los Angeles and Curator of Southeast Asian Art at Los Angeles County Museum of Art. Two recent publications include edited books: *Art from Thailand* 1999 and *Roots of Tantra* 2001.

Nagaraja Rao is a Ph.D. in Archaeology from Poona. He was Director of Archaeology and Museums in Karnataka and Director General and Archaeological Survey of India, New Delhi. He is editor of *Vijayanagara: Progress of Research 1979-1983,* 1983, *Vijayanagara: Progress of Research 1983-1984*, 1985.

Indu Parthasarthy has a Ph.D. in Art History, Bangalore University, India. She has taught Art History at the Natya Institute of Kathak and Choreography, Mount Carmel College and the Chitrakala Parishath College of Fine Arts, Bangalore. She conducted research for the Crafts Council of Karnataka, entitled 'Wood in Karnataka' funded by the Government of India.

Anila Verghese is historian and Principal of Sophia College for Women, Mumbai, India. Publications: *Religious Traditions at Vijayanagara: as Revealed through its Monuments 1995, Sculpture at Vijayanagara: Iconography and Style* joint author with Dr. Anna L. Dallapiccola, 1998 and *Archaeology, Art and Religion: New Perspectives on Vijayanagara,* 2000.

Gerard Foekema is Ph.D. in Art and Architecture History from Leiden University, The Netherlands. He has dedicated his life to the art and architecture of the Chalukya and Hoysala temples in South India. His collection of about 50,000 photographs and slides is only second to that of the American Institute of Indian Studies, New Delhi and Philadelphia.

Nalini Rao is Professor of World Art at Soka University of America, CA. She holds a Ph.D. in Art History from the University of California, Los Angeles and a Ph.D. in Ancient History from the University of Mysore. Her publications include, *Boundaries and Transformations* 1997, *Contours of Modernity* 2005 joint author with Debashish Banerji and *Royal Artistic Imagery at Vijayanagara* (forthcoming).

Deepak Shimkhada has a Ph.D. from Claremont Graduate University, Ca and is Assistant Professor, Religious Studies in Claremont McKenna College, Ca. He has published many articles and his books include *Popular Buddhist Mantras in Sanskrit,* 1985 joint author with Shih Pei Lai and edited *Himalayas at the Crossroads: Portrait of a Changing World,* 1987.

S.R.Rao has D.Litt and was Emeritus Scientist and Archaeologist, National Institute of Oceanography and Superintending Archaeologist, ASI and a Nehru fellow. Some of his works include *Lothal and the Indus Civilization* 1973, *The Decipherment of the Indus Script,* Bombay 1982 and *Dawn and Devolution of the Indus Civilization* 1991.

Subhash Kak received his Ph.D from the Indian Institute of Technology, Delhi. He is Delaune Distinguished Professor of Electrical Engineering and Professor of Asian Studies and of Cognitive Science at Louisiana State University, Baton Rouge. Author of fifteen books his recent ones are *The Astronomical Code of the Rgveda* 2000, *The Asvamedha* 2002, *The Gods Within* 2002, and *The Architecture of Knowledge* 2004.

Aparna Raghunathan earned her a M.A. in Landscape Architecture, University of Illinois Urbana Champaign and a B.A in Architecture from Regional Engineering College, Tiruchirapalli. She has worked on residential, garden designs, planned communities, amusement parks, recreation centers, club house designs and health care projects.

Amita Sinha received her Ph.D. from University of California, Berkeley in 1989 and joined the faculty in the Department of Landscape Architecture,

University of Illinois at Urbana Champaign. Her forthcoming book is *Landscapes in India: Forms and Meanings* from University Press of Colorado.

Choodamani Nandagopal has a Ph.D. from Mysore University. She was a Senior Fellow in the American Institute of Indian Studies, Nehru Fellow Victoria and Albert Museum, London. She has authored the book *Dance and Music in Temple Architecture* 1990 and *Temple Jewellery* 1997 along with Vatsala Iyengar.